Stages in a Life

24. Dez. 1837.
10. September 1898.

GEWIDMET VON DER K. K. REICHSHAUPT- UND RESIDENZSTADT WIEN.

Stages in a Life

Edited by
Brigitte Hamann and Elisabeth Hassmann

Verlag Christian Brandstätter · Vienna–Munich

With 270 illustrations

Companion publication to the exhibition
Elisabeth, Eternal Beauty
at Schönbrunn Palace and the Hofburg, Vienna
April 2nd 1998 to February 16th 1999
organised by the Schloss Schönbrunn
Kultur- und Betriebsgesellschaft m. b. H.

First published in January 1998

Original idea and editing by Elisabeth Hassmann
Original layout design by Bohatsch und Schedler
Graphic design, type-setting and
reproduction by Armanda and Geisler
Translated by Sophie Kidd
Printed by Grasl Druck & Neue Medien in Bad Vöslau.
Typeset in Utopia

Cover illustration: Empress Elisabeth of Austria, copy by
E. Riegele, 1923 (Collection of Prince Thurn und Taxis, Regensburg)
after the painting by Franz Xaver Winterhalter, 1864 (private collection).
The painting shows Elisabeth at the age of 26 wearing a peignoir,
her face lit by the morning sun. Franz Joseph had Winterhalter's painting
set up facing his writing-desk in the Vienna Hofburg.

ISBN 3-85447-796-1

Schloss Schönbrunn
Kultur- und Betriebsges. m. b. H.
A-1130 Vienna, Schloss Schönbrunn

Contents

The stages in the empress's life

Elisabeth in 1855;
painting by Franz
Schrotzberg (Sacher
Hotel, Vienna).

The empress at the
age of 25; painting
by Franz Schrotz-
berg (Wittelsbacher
Ausgleichfonds,
Munich).

Elisabeth in a
peignoir; copy by
E. Riegele, 1923
(Prince Thurn und
Taxis, Regensburg),
after a painting by
Franz Xaver Winter-
halter, 1864 (private
collection).

Elisabeth against the evening sky; painting by Franz Xaver Winterhalter, 1864 (Hofburg, Vienna).

The empress in a ball gown with diamond stars in her hair; painting by Franz Xaver Winterhalter, 1864 (Hofburg, Vienna).

Posthumous portrait of the empress; painting by Gyula Benczúr, 1898/99 (National Museum of Hungary, Budapest).

The course of Elisabeth's life

Brigitte Hamann

Elisabeth's brothers and sisters on the terrace at Possenhofen; from l. to r.: Sophie, Max Emanuel, Carl Theodor, Helene, Ludwig Wilhelm, Mathilde and Marie; painting by Joseph Stieler, 1854 (private collection).

In the beginning was a childhood and a youth that Elisabeth was to mourn like a lost paradise for the rest of her life.

Called Sisi by her family, Elisabeth grew up as the third of eight handsome and self-willed children of Duke Max of Bavaria. Since the duke's family belonged to a collateral branch of the Wittelsbach family and thus had no official function at the royal court in Munich, it could afford to live a purely private life. Duke Max occupied his time with his personal interests, playing the zither, collecting Bavarian folksongs, adding to his celebrated library, writing a little poetry and travelling extensively. He had intellectual friends, mostly from bourgeois circles, indulged in numerous affairs and sired illegitimate children. He was fond of playing the scourge of the aristocracy, affecting to sympathise with revolutionary sentiments.

The »Palais Max« in the Ludwigsstrasse in Munich, where Elisabeth was born on December 24th 1837, was remarkable less for aristocratic splendour than for its bohemian atmosphere. As well as a *café chantant* on Parisian lines there was a ballroom with risqué murals. In a circus manège on the ground floor, the master of the house occasionally performed as a circus-rider, surrounded by riotous clown acts and military spectacles, to the horror of Munich high society but the great entertainment of his children.

Duchess Ludovika, Elisabeth's mother and sister of Archduchess Sophie, with her children Ludwig, Helene and the new-born Elisabeth; lithograph by Ernst Kaiser, 1838.

Duke Maximilian of Bavaria, Elisabeth's father, after a painting from 1888.

The eleven-year-old Sisi with her favourite brother, Carl Theodor, nick-named Gackel; in the background is Lake Starnberg; gouache, signed and dated Carl Haag, 1849 (Rebasso Collection, Vienna).

Elisabeth's adored mother, Ludovika, looked after her children herself, despite the fact that this was unheard of for a member of the aristocracy who was, moreover, a daughter of the Bavarian king, Maximilian I, and a sister of the powerful Archduchess Sophie in Vienna. Ludovika's small retinue had not been chosen according to conventional aristocratic criteria and was treated as part of the family.

The ducal summer residence at Possenhofen was small and modest by aristocratic standards. Its main attraction lay in its beautiful natural setting, on the banks of Lake Starnberg, overlooking the Roseninsel (Rose Island). Here the family lived surrounded by nature; the children learned to fish, hike and ride. They had many pets, played with the children of the local peasantry and spoke Bavarian dialect. Teachers and priests had little authority in this household.

Thus the upbringing of the duke's children was (according to courtly opinion) extremely unsatisfactory. Only the eldest daughter,

Helene, received a thorough education, with special emphasis on religious instruction. She was promised to her cousin, the young Emperor Franz Joseph of Austria, the most sought-after match in Europe and ruler over an empire of 40 million souls.

When Helene reached the age of 18, the betrothal ceremony was to take place in private at the spa resort of Bad Ischl in the Salzkammergut, where the emperor would celebrate his 23rd birthday on August 18th, 1853. Mother and daughter set off accompanied by a small retinue (though very wisely without Duke Max). Since their second daughter, 15-year-old Sisi, was of marriageable age and Franz Joseph had three younger brothers, she was also allowed to join the party.

The story of the betrothal is legendary: Franz Joseph only had eyes for little Sisi, the wrong sister. He took no heed of the horrified expressions of mother and aunt, nor of Helene's tears. Archduchess Sophie later wrote of this moment: »The dear little thing had no idea of the deep impression she had made on Franzi. Until the moment her mother spoke to her about it, she was filled only with the timidity and shyness inspired by the many people around her.«

Franz Joseph, then an attractive, wiry young man with fair hair and blue eyes, and a connoisseur of women, treated the bewildered child with the long brown plaits with tender consideration. In order to amuse her, he had a swing put up in the garden.

On the day of the betrothal, the party made an excursion to Hallstatt, where Franz Joseph explained the sights of his favourite landscape to her. This love of nature was one of the few things the couple had in common. A memorial plaque at the Post Hotel, where the party dined, commemorates the occasion.

The imperial bride, decked out for the first time in her life with precious jewels, was hailed by the population with patriotic jubilation and fireworks. Archduchess Sophie presented the young couple with a summer residence in Bad Ischl, the ground plan of which was extended to form the letter E. This imperial villa is today in the possession of one of the couple's great-grand-children.

Emperor Franz Joseph in the robes of the Order of the Golden Fleece; lithograph by Gabriel Decker after the painting by Anton Einsle, 1853.

Elisabeth holding the bridal wreath presented to her by Franz Joseph at Christmas 1853 as a gift from his mother; coloured lithograph by Franz Hanfstengel.

The course of Elisabeth's life

Elisabeth's depart-ure from Munich at the Triumphal Arch on April 20th 1854 ; lithograph by Anton Ziegler.

Looking back on this time, Elisabeth later wrote: »Marriage is an absurd institution. One is sold as a 15-year-old child and makes a vow one does not understand and then regrets for 30 years or more, and which one can never again undo.«

In the few months before the wedding the young Sisi had a huge amount to learn: Austrian history, French, Italian and Czech, courtly protocol and courtly dancing as well as conversation, among many other things. The young girl's fear of life in Vienna, the imperial capital and residence, grew daily and culminated in the timorous wish uttered of her bridegroom: »Oh, if only he were a tailor!«

In the early morning of April 20th 1854, the 16-year-old bride of the emperor set off on the journey from Munich to Vienna in a six-horse open carriage, followed by her parents, brothers and sisters, ladies-in-waiting and maids. At midday they stopped to rest in Landshut. There people were waiting to offer their congratulations, led by the mayor, the priest, a brass band and little girls with bouquets of flowers. The bride had to listen patiently to all the speeches, make a graceful reply, and endure being the focus of many curious eyes. Scenes such as this were to characterise Elisabeth's public life from now onwards. Shy, fearful and highly sensitive by nature, Elisabeth would always find her official duties as empress a burden.

From Landshut the journey continued on to Straubing and thus to the next festive reception. Here, after spending the night at the Black Bear Hotel, the bridal party embarked on the Danube paddle-steamer *City of Regensburg* which brought them to Passau on the Bavarian-Austrian border in the early afternoon. A memorial tablet commemorates the imperial bride's tearful leave-taking of Bavaria.

On the evening of April 21st, the boat docked at Linz, the first stop in Austria. To the joyful surprise of the young girl, who was already severely overtired, the emperor joined them on board here in order to lead his bride onto Austrian soil himself, before the official reception in Vienna. Franz Joseph can hardly be accused of a lack of sensitivity at that period.

The bedchamber of the emperor's bride in the Landhaus at Linz. The blue furnishings (blue being the colour of Bavaria) and the rose pattern of the carpet must have been a deliberate reference to the bride, who was known as the »Rose of Bavaria«; gouache by Joseph Maria Kaiser, 1854 (Historical Museum of the City of Vienna).

Elisabeth arriving at Nussdorf near Vienna on April 22nd 1854 on the paddle steamer »Franz Joseph«; in the background is a triumphal arch erected for the welcoming ceremony; lithograph by Vinzenz Katzler.

In Linz a wooden pavilion decorated with bunting had been prepared, where local dignitaries and guests of honour were waiting, accompanied by the obligatory young girls dressed in festive white. In the main square there were a triumphal arch and stands for the spectators – and again countless speeches followed by a performance by the »Frohsinn« choral society. The Linz theatre put on a gala performance of *Die Rosen der Elisabeth* (The Roses of Elisabeth). The long day was concluded by festive illuminations and a torchlight procession. The bridal party spent what was left of the night at the Upper Austrian Landhaus. The emperor departed for Vienna the next morning at 4.30 am in order to arrive in time for the official reception in the capital.

At Linz the Bavarian party transferred to an Austrian boat, the most magnificent vessel ever to have sailed down the Danube: the paddle-steamer *Franz Joseph*, decorated with flowers and bunting. It conveyed the bride in a triumphal procession to Vienna, hailed from the banks by thousands of loyal subjects. But the bride, instead of looking forward full of pride and anticipation to her glorious future, became ever quieter and more nervous. It was clear that the strenuous journey had only been a small foretaste of all the festivities that were in store for her. Sisi was more afraid than she had ever been.

The thunder of cannons and the pealing of all Vienna's church bells heralded the arrival of the emperor's bride at the landing stage in Nussdorf, while curious onlookers crowded the banks right up to the slopes of the Leopoldsberg. After a lengthy welcoming ceremony, the procession of carriages drove to Schönbrunn for yet more festivities. Everything terrified the 16-year-old girl: the palace with its more than a thousand rooms, the numerous footmen, the uniformed guards at every door, the omnipresent protocol, the disapproving looks of the new *Obersthofmeisterin* (the mistress of the empress's household, the highest office at court). But what frightened her more than anything was the all-powerful figure of the real empress of Austria: Archduchess Sophie.

On April 23rd, as the young bride entered Vienna in a state carriage drawn by eight Lipizzaner horses (opening the newly-constructed Elisabeth Bridge across the River Wien on her way), the Viennese lining the streets to welcome their future empress were astounded to see a timorous child dissolved in tears.

The wedding, which took place on April 24th in the Augustinerkirche (Church of the Augustine Brethren), was celebrated by the Archbishop of Vienna together with more than 70 bishops and prelates. It was followed by eight days of festivities. Elisabeth's family and their attendants then returned to Bavaria, leaving Elisabeth to begin her new life as Empress of Austria.

Wedding ceremony in the Augustiner-kirche in Vienna on April 24th 1854; Cardinal Rauscher blesses the young couple; anonymous lithograph.

The course of Elisabeth's life

Wir
MAXIMILIAN II.
von Gottes Gnaden
Koenig von Bayern
Pfalzgraf bey Rhein
Herzog von Bayern, Franken und in Schwaben &c. &c.
Urkunden und bekennen hiermit:

Da Wir nach vorhergegangenem freundschaftlichen Benehmen mit Seiner Apostolischen Majestaet dem Kaiser Franz Joseph I von Oesterreich, Koenig von Ungarn und Böhmen &c. ... Elisabeth Amalie Eugenie Herzogin in Bayern Königliche Hoheit ...

Marriage contract dated March 4th 1854 (Haus-, Hof- und Staatsarchiv, Vienna).

Elisabeth at the age of 17; painting by Franz Schrotzberg, dated 1855 (Sacher Hotel, Vienna).

The young couple riding in the game park at Lainz; a love of riding was one of the few interests shared by the emperor and his wife; lithograph by Eduard Kaiser, 1855.

The situation in the Crimea and continuing upheavals in the Balkans made an uninterrupted honeymoon impossible. The newly-wedded couple drove to Laxenburg Palace near Vienna, but as the sole monarch, Franz Joseph had to drive to Vienna early each day to see to the affairs of state and did not return until late in the evening. His 16-year-old wife was left on her own, desperately homesick and isolated in a large circle of totally strange people, who stood by to attend to her needs and instruct her in court protocol.

It was a beautiful spring and Laxenburg Palace was an ideal setting for days of love, standing as it did on an artificial lake in a pretty landscaped park. But it was here that the lonely young girl wrote her poem entitled *Longing*:

> *But what is the joy of spring to me,*
> *Here in this far-off alien land?*
> *I long for the sun of my home country*
> *I long for River Isar's banks.*

And a fortnight after the wedding, on May 8th 1854:

> *Oh, had I but never left the path*
> *That would have led me to Freedom!*
> *Oh, had I never strayed*
> *Onto the broad avenues of vanity!*
>
> *I have awakened in a dungeon*
> *With fetters on my wrists.*
> *And my longing ever stronger –*
> *And Freedom! thou, turned away from me!*
>
> *I have awakened from a trance*
> *That held my spirit captive,*
> *And rail in vain at this exchange*
> *By which, oh Freedom, I thee lost!*

Elisabeth continued to hate Vienna and life at court, all the more as the elegant ladies of the aristocracy looked down on the awkward, shy young empress, who, according to the view of the ladies-in-waiting, was incapable of learning anything

The imperial family in 1860 at Schönbrunn on the terrace of the Kavalier tract. Standing from l. to r.: Franz Joseph, Ferdinand Max with his wife, Charlotte, Ludwig Viktor and Karl Ludwig, the emperor's brothers; seated from l. to r.: Elisabeth with Rudolf and Gisela, Sophie and Franz Karl, the emperor's parents; photograph by Ludwig Angerer.

and must therefore be stupid. The emperor was preoccupied with affairs of state and entrusted his young bride to the vigorous hands of his mother.

Elisabeth became a silent, morose young woman who was devoted to her husband and otherwise had few contacts. However, she fulfilled her main duty of bearing healthy heirs for the House of Habsburg. After two girls, of whom only the second, Gisela, survived to adulthood, she at last gave birth to Crown Prince Rudolf in 1858, an intelligent, imaginative and extremely sensitive child. Citing the inexperience and youth of the empress, Archduchess Sophie assumed responsibility for the upbringing of the children and the running of the nurseries. Thus Elisabeth had little chance to make a home for herself in Vienna as the mother of her children and in this way gain confidence.

In his excessive admiration for his mother, Franz Joseph was unable to stand up for his young wife against Archduchess Sophie. Tired of domestic squabbles, after five years of marriage he sought comfort in other arms, or so court gossip had it. When this came to Elisabeth's ears, she lost her nerve and fled from Vienna to Possenhofen in July 1860. She was in such haste that she used the new railway between Vienna and Munich (the Empress Elisabeth Western Railway) before it had been officially opened. She had not seen her home for more than six years.

It was a long time before she could finally be persuaded to return to Vienna, and once there she immediately became ill. She refused to eat, suffered from claustrophobia and fits of crying, and grew daily weaker. She could only think of escape and refused point-blank to remain on imperial soil. She voiced a wish of travelling to the island of Madeira in the Atlantic, of which Archduke Maximilian, her favourite brother-in-law, had given her enthusiastic descriptions. Eventually, since her condition was life-threatening, her physicians agreed. At this time Gisela and Rudolf were four and two years old respectively.

Elisabeth playing the macheta with her ladies-in-waiting Countess Karoline Hunyady, Princess Windisch-grätz and Princess Helene Taxis on Madeira in 1860; photograph.

In November 1860, the 22-year-old empress set off incognito on her journey. She travelled via Bamberg, where she took leave of Franz Joseph, Frankfurt and Mainz to Antwerp. There she embarked for Madeira together with a small, hand-picked retinue of 27 people, staying on the island until the end of April 1861.

Here, in the seclusion of a remote island, far from the dreary Austrian politics of that era, free from her mother-in-law's attempts to make her conform and from obligations of every kind, surrounded by people who admired her (and furnished with unlimited credit) Elisabeth recovered her health.

Once back in Vienna, the old symptoms returned within four days: she refused to eat, had crying fits, a severe cough, complained of pain and became increasingly frail. Her personal physician prescribed an immediate return to warmer climes, warning that she would not last longer than six weeks in Vienna. This time the journey went via Miramar near Trieste, where Archduke Maximilian joined the travelling party, to Corfu, at that time still under British rule. Hardly had the sea voyage begun when the patient began to display a hearty appetite. The opinion at the Viennese court was that the empress was neurotic rather than consumptive; there was no sympathy to be reckoned with from that quarter.

Although Elisabeth longed to see her children, she did not want to return to Vienna. She thus insisted on a stay of several months in Venice, which was at that time still under Austrian rule. The children – Gisela, now aged five, and Rudolf, now aged three – were sent to her in the charge of a retinue.

The empress stayed in Venice until May 1862, but did not return to Vienna, travelling instead directly to Reichenau on the Rax, where the children spent the summer at the Rudolf Villa. From there Elisabeth went to take the waters at the spa resort of Bad Kissingen in Bavaria, afterwards travelling on to Possenhofen. It was not until her father finally put his foot down that she returned to Vienna unexpectedly on

Elisabeth with her dogs in Venice in 1862; photograph by A. Golla.

Elisabeth and her two children Gisela and Rudolf with their governess Charlotte von Welden in Venice in 1862; pen-and-ink drawing by Emil Hartizsch, 1862.

August 18th 1862, Franz Joseph's birthday, after an absence of nearly two years.

It was clear to everyone that the twenty-four-year-old Elisabeth was a different woman: self-confident, forceful, demanding – and above all, a woman who had blossomed into an extraordinary beauty. Franz Joseph became her most ardent and humbly devoted admirer. From now on, she had her way in everything she wanted. And what she wanted above all was to travel wherever she liked, as long as it took her away from Vienna.

There had never been much in the way of traditional family life in this marriage, and what little there had been disappeared completely after this.

The further the fame of her beauty and grace spread in the world, the more Elisabeth realised that this beauty meant power. She did everything to preserve this power, her claim to being the most beautiful queen in the world. She made a thorough-going cult of her beauty, with obsessive exercising, riding and hiking, starvation diets, all kinds of bathing cures and frequent stays at spa resorts, but above all with the inordinate amount of time spent in caring for her knee-length chestnut brown hair. Whenever she felt that she was not looking her best, she cancelled all her engagements, a habit to which an increasing number of people took exception.

Her famous, hard-earned beauty and her unrelenting hatred of the court at Vienna reinforced an innate egocentricity and narcissism which Elisabeth now indulged in to the full.

Elisabeth was now in her late twenties and at the height of her self-confidence when she became politically active for the first and last time in her life. This was in connection with Hungary, abhorred by Archduchess Sophie on account of its rebellious tendencies. Elisabeth had been to Hungary for the first time on an official visit with the emperor in 1857, and had conceived an immediate liking for the country. Over the years she gathered an increasing number of Hungarians round her, and began systematically (and with great success) to learn Hungarian, thereby scandalising Sophie, who saw the Hungarians

as revolutionaries and treacherous rebels against the House of Habsburg.

In January 1866, the 28-year-old empress met the 42-year-old Hungarian politician and former revolutionary Count Gyula Andrássy, who invited the imperial couple in the name of the Hungarian nation to visit Budapest. This visit was to last five weeks and intensified Elisabeth's love for the country. Increasingly, the empress became Andrássy's political tool and began to influence her devoted husband to the former's advantage.

In 1866, when the Prussian army was at the gates of Vienna following Austria's defeat at Königgrätz, Elisabeth sought refuge with her children in Budapest (while Archduchess Sophie chose to go to Bad Ischl), remaining there two months, and was in constant contact with Hungarian politicians. After a protracted tug-of-war, the Hungarian faction supporting Ferenc Deák and

Elisabeth, King Ludwig II of Bavaria and the Tsar and Tsarina of Russia in front of the hydro in Bad Kissingen, 1864; watercolour signed Joh. Maar (Historical Museum of the City of Vienna).

Gyula Andrássy achieved its goal on June 8th 1867: Franz Joseph was crowned King of Hungary in the Cathedral of St. Matthew in Budapest, thus guaranteeing the old Hungarian constitution. The Austrian Empire had became the Dual Monarchy of Austria-Hungary. Elisabeth, the crowned and acclaimed queen of Hungary, was at the zenith of her life.

Grateful that the emperor had granted her wishes, Elisabeth agreed to bear him another child. Marie Valerie was born in Budapest ten months after the coronation and was brought up as a little Hungarian girl, with Elisabeth having sole responsibility for her upbringing.

As a gift from the Hungarian nation to mark the coronation, the royal couple were presented with the Baroque Gödöllő Palace near Budapest, which was surrounded by a spacious park and wooded countryside, an ideal place for hunting. From now on, Elisabeth spent a good part of the year here as a »Hungarian«, together with her »Hungarian« child and Hungarian friends.

The louder the critical voices in Vienna became, the more Elisabeth hated the Hofburg and Schönbrunn. Now, however, she could be sure of her husband's support. He funded her travelling in luxury, an activity that was becoming ever more comfortable due to the expansion of the European railway network. The empress had her own special train to transport her 60-strong retinue in a manner befitting her rank. Her retinue included her *Obersthofmeisterin*, ladies-in-waiting, ladies' maids, a physician, secretaries, bathing women, hairdressers, cooks and coachmen, grooms, stablehands and kennelboys, not forgetting the horses, dogs and carriages. The special train was followed by a goods train which transported all the baggage.

When she was not in Hungary, Elisabeth was usually in Bavaria, especially during the early summer. In order to be near her family, Possenhofen being much too small, she hired the Strauch Hotel in Feldafing on Lake Starnberg, close to her family home. Here this otherwise shy and retiring woman enjoyed entertaining visitors, her parents and seven brothers and sisters together with their families, as well as King Ludwig II of Bavaria, who was becoming increasingly eccentric.

She had this Bavarian hotel extended to accommodate all her requirements for luxury: a kitchen was added for her own

Franz Joseph and Crown Prince Rudolf on a visit to Elisabeth at Merano, watching a riflemen's festival on April 10th 1871; wood engraving after a drawing by Franz Kollartz.

cooks, together with stabling for her horses. Little Marie Valerie with her governesses and tutors had to have rooms opening onto the garden. The empress insisted on having her own exercise room even here, together with a spiral staircase to give her private access to the garden. Annexes were built for her guests. Whenever the empress was in residence, the other hotel guests – even including the illustrious Baron Rothschild – naturally had to make do with the annexes.

The empress frequently visited her brothers and sisters: in 1865 she travelled to the wedding of her favourite brother, Carl Theodor, in Dresden. In 1867 she went to Zurich to be with her sister Mathilde Trani for the birth of the latter's first child, and in 1869 to Rome for the confinement of her sister Marie, who at that time was living in exile at her Roman residence, the Villa Farnese. During this stay, Elisabeth also witnessed the opening ceremony of the Vatican Council, but could not bear to stay longer than an hour. She described the visit of the Pope to the Villa Farnese in a letter to Franz Joseph in disrespectful terms and complained – once again – about the »dreadful ceremonies«. The undoubted highlight of her visit to Rome was a hunt in aristocratic company in the campagna.

One example illustrating the extent of the empress's absences from Vienna is the period from October 1870 to May 1872: from October 17th 1870 to June 1871 she was at Trautmannsdorff Castle near Merano with Gisela and Marie, afterwards travelling to Bavaria and on to Bad Ischl. From October 1871 to May 1872, she was in Merano again, where she was visited by her sisters.

Elisabeth's journeys became much more complicated and expensive when she started to concentrate exclusively on her

Examples of the »portrait tableaux« of the emperor and empress which were popular as postcards.

The course of Elisabeth's life

Elisabeth jumping a hedge in her much-admired close-fitting riding habit; steel engraving by T. L. Atkinson (Hofburg, Vienna) after a painting by John C. Charleton (private collection), c. 1880/82.

riding in the 1870s. At first she trained at Gödöllő with the best instructors, but also took lessons from circus-riders. Like her father in Munich, she had a circus ring built at Gödöllő for her circus-riding tricks, and the Empress of Austria eventually became proficient at jumping through two hoops on horseback. She rode with the famous aristocratic hunts of the monarchy, in Hungary, Göding in Moravia (with Prince Liechtenstein's hunt), and in Pardubitz in Bohemia (with the Larisch hunt). At short notice, she cancelled her official state engagements at the World Exhibition in Vienna in 1873 and travelled to Payerbach on the Rax to rest.

In 1874 she spent the hunting season in England with her best horses, this time, however, still mainly as a spectator. In 1875 she trained at Sassetôt in Normandy, where she had a serious riding accident. From there she went to Paris, where she jumped the hurdles in the Bois du Boulogne.

In 1876, after training with Captain »Bay« Middleton, she rode with an English hunt, staying for weeks at the Easton Neston estate near Towcester. In 1878 she stayed at Cottesbrooke, also in Northamptonshire. In 1879 and 1880 she participated in the even more dangerous hunts in Ireland, which, in view of the anti-English unrest there, strained relations with Queen Victoria. On her way back from Ireland in 1880, she broke her journey in Brussels for four hours to attend the betrothal of Crown Prince Rudolf. In 1881 and 1882, out of political considerations, she contented herself with hunting in England (at Combermere in Cheshire).

Both in England and in Ireland, she had costly alterations made to the mansions she had rented for just a few weeks, including exercise rooms, spiral staircases, extra stabling, railway sidings for the transport of her horses and an extra waiting room at the station. The purchase of expensive racehorses consumed horrendous sums of money, but Franz Joseph remained generous to the last.

Elisabeth was 44 years old when rheumatism began to make itself felt. In 1882 she suddenly cancelled plans for her next hunting trip. That year she even accompanied her husband on an official state visit to Trieste for the celebrations marking the fifth centenary of the city's affiliation to the House of Habsburg, despite the real risk of assassination.

Having given up riding, Elisabeth now concentrated on fencing. In order to take lessons from the famous fencing master Friedrich Schulze, she travelled to Heidelberg, where the Schlosshotel equipped a special fencing room for her private use. Here as everywhere, she went on long hikes, such as the famous »Philosophers' Way«, and proved herself a keen student of culture, visiting the nearby fortress of Rheinstein, the Niederwald monument, Heilbronn, Worms, Trier, Coblenz, Schloss Stolzenfels and the ruins at Ebersteinburg.

Another attempt by Elisabeth to maintain a separate individual identity as distinct from her position as empress found expression in the poetry she wrote during the 1880s, which was heavily influenced by the poet she most admired, Heinrich Heine. She visited Heine's grave in Paris and called on his sister in Hamburg. She donated a large sum to the fund for erecting a monument to the poet in Düsseldorf, for which Emperor Wilhelm II subsequently refused to give permission. She became completely bound up in her fantasies, claimed to have spiritualistic contact with Heine and saw herself as Titania from Shakespeare's *Midsummer Night's Dream*, her favourite play.

In her poems she reveals her loneliness, fear of people and her contempt for court life. They also express her great love of nature, whether in connection with Greece or the North Sea *(Nordseelieder)*.

At certain places in particularly beautiful landscapes in Greece, Switzerland and Bavaria there are still memorial tablets to Empress Elisabeth. In some spa resorts there are »Elisabeth fountains«. In Bad Langenschwalbach in the Taunus mountains, for example, there is an Elisabeth Temple at the top of the Busemach mountain commemorating the hikes she went on there with Christomanos, her Greek companion and tutor.

There are naturally many memorial tablets in Austria and Hungary. A hike she went on together with her husband up the Grossglocker (Austria's highest mountain) during the early years of their marriage is attested by the names »Franz-Josephs-Höhe« (Hoher Sattel) and »Elisabethruhe« (Laretterboden), as well as their signatures in an entry dated September 1856 in the book kept in the refuge near the top of the Grossglockner. In Styria the area around the imperial hunting lodge at Mürzsteg or near Mariazell were favourite destinations for excursions. In 1883, while riding on the Totes Weib mountain in Styria, the rotten planks of a wooden bridge collapsed underneath horse and rider; only a passing woodsman saved the empress from plunging into the abyss.

It is above all the Salzkammergut which has the greatest number of memorials to the empress. Elisabeth frequently

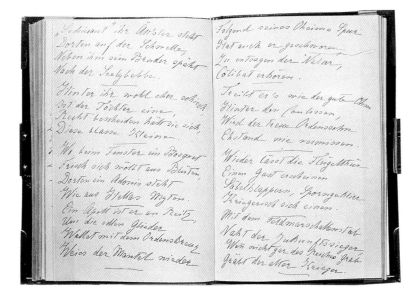

Elisabeth's »diary in poems« (Swiss Federal Archives, Berne).

Incident on the Tote Weib mountain near Mürzsteg (Styria) in the summer of 1883; anonymous wood engraving.

climbed the Jainzen mountain near Ischl, loved hiking to Gosau Mill in Hallstatt, took parties to the Rettenbachalm, to the Almsee lake, to Gmunden, and to the imperial hunting lodges on the Langbathsee and Offensee lakes. In 1884 she signed the visitors' book in the refuge near the summit of the Loser mountain. On the Hütteneck mountain she had her own little »viewing hut« from 1881. In August 1885 she exhibited similar eccentric behaviour to her cousin, Ludwig II of Bavaria, by insisting on climbing the Schmittenhöhe at night, starting from Zell am See at 1.40 am and arriving at the summit at 6 in the morning, accompanied by mountain guides carrying lanterns.

The countryside around Vienna also has its share of memorials to the empress: the Kaiserbründl (imperial fountain) near Pressbaum, commemorative tablets in Kaltenleutgeben

Emperor Wilhelm I
and Elisabeth leav-
ing the hydro in
Gastein; here Elisa-
beth is not conceal-
ing her face with
a fan or veil, as
was her custom
as she grew older;
photograph by
Max Balde, 1886.

and Tullnerbach, a memorial column on the Bisamberg »*dedicated in deep respect by the women of Korneuburg and its
environs*«.

Elisabeth attempted to alleviate the growing complaints
of old age with forced marches in all weathers and all sorts of
cures. She rented 40 rooms at the Doelen Hotel in Amsterdam
for massage treatment for rheumatism with the famous physician Dr. Johann Mezger. When the doctor started treating
patients in Baden-Baden and then in Wiesbaden, she took
cures in those resorts as well.

Franz Joseph's attempts to keep his wife in Vienna were
all unsuccessful, even when he made her the gift of a splendid
hunting lodge designed by Hasenauer, one of the Ringstrasse
architects, in the huge natural park at Lainz. She named it the
Hermes Villa and furnished it to her taste. A further attempt
to make her settle down somewhere, if not in Vienna, was the
building of the Achilleion on Corfu, dedicated to Elisabeth's
favourite hero, Achilles. However, no sooner was it finished

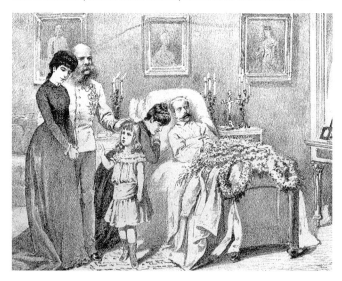

Elisabeth, Franz
Joseph and Crown
Princess Stephanie
at Rudolf's death-
bed; wood engrav-
ing after a drawing
by Theodor Breid-
wiser, 1889.

than Elisabeth lost all interest in her possession, preferring to stay at hotels when she was travelling.

The suicide of her son Rudolf at Mayerling in January 1889 came as a complete shock, a shock exacerbated by pangs of conscience. Rudolf had adored his mother and had waited in vain his whole life for her affection. She had never truly loved him. When this tragedy hit her, she was 51 years old, obviously affected by the change of life, severely depressed, desperate, extremely unsociable and full of inner disquiet. Her legendary beauty had faded, her skin was wrinkled, her sight blurred.

The emperor and empress with their family, 1888; lithograph by M. Streicher.

ERZHERZOGIN MARIA VALERIA.

KRONPRINZ
ERZHERZOG RUDOLPH.

KRONPRINZESSIN
ERZHERZOGIN STEPHANIE.

ERZHERZOG FRANZ KARL.

ERZHERZOGIN SOPHIE.

Sr. Majestät Kaiser Franz Josef I.

Jhre Majestät Kaiserin Elisabeth

HERZOG MAXIMILIAN JOSEPH IN BAYERN.

HERZOGIN LUDOVICA WILHELMINE IN BAYERN.

HERZOG LEOPOLD VON BAYERN.

ERZHERZOGIN GISELA HERZOGIN VON BAYERN.

The last photograph of Elisabeth and Franz Joseph together, taken as they were promenading in Luitpold Park at Bad Kissingen between April 25th and May 5th 1898; photograph by Kolb.

The last photograph of Elisabeth: the empress and her lady-in-waiting Countess Irma Sztáray in Territet on September 3rd 1898.

Apart from hiking for hours she was unable to engage in any sports. Now she gave up writing poetry and considered suicide. Rumours that the empress was mentally ill circulated in Vienna. However, she did introduce the actress Katharina Schratt to her increasingly lonely husband, thus initiating a close and devoted friendship, an act that won her the eternal gratefulness of both the actress and the emperor.

The empress spent the last nine years of her life as if she had no real home. As a *mater dolorosa*, always dressed in black and mostly accompanied by only one lady-in-waiting and a single manservant, she travelled unceasingly back and forth across Europe. Although she was informed about the risk of assassination, she always refused to take a security agent with her.

Both Hungary and Greece had lost their attraction for her. Now she travelled from one spa resort to another, preferring to stay at the vast late-nineteenth century hotels which offered their guests splendid views, such as the Bellvue in Rigi, the Jungfrauenblick in Interlaken, the Schweizerhof at the waterfalls on the Rhine at Schaffhausen or the Grand Hotel in Territet (Caux) on Lake Geneva. In large cities she preferred the international hotels which guaranteed her a certain degree of anonymity, such as the Baur au Lac in Zurich, the Beau Rivage in Geneva and the Hotel d'Europe in Venice, among others.

In March 1898 she travelled to Territet, from there to Bad Kissingen in April, moving on to take the waters in Bad Brückenau in mid-June, then from there to Vienna and Ischl, where she joined the emperor. On July 15th she travelled from Ischl to see her brothers and sisters in Munich, paying her customary visit to the Hofbräuhaus in order to drink her beloved Munich beer. She then went on to Bad Nauheim, where she took the waters for six weeks until the end of August, which did much to restore her strength. Afterwards she departed for Territet (Caux) for a four-week cure in the late summer of 1898. Here she undertook excursions to Rocher de Nay as well as Evian-les-Bains and Ouchy, near Lausanne.

From Territet Elisabeth took the steamer across the lake to Geneva on September 9th, in order from there to pay a private

visit to Baroness Julie Rothschild in Pregny. She was accompanied only by a lady-in-waiting, Countess Sztáray, and a manservant, who carried the ladies' overcoats and a handbag. The afternoon passed harmoniously, with good food and a walk around the famous Rothschild gardens, including a visit to the orchid hothouses.

In the early evening the empress's party returned to Geneva, where Elisabeth paid one of her habitual visits to her favourite confectioner's and purchased toys for her grandchildren. She stayed the night at the Beau Rivage. The following morning she planned to take the steamer back to Montreux. On the way to the landing stage, Elisabeth was stabbed with a sharpened file by an assassin, the Italian anarchist Luigi Lucheni. He dealt a violent death to the empress, who was depressed and weary of life, yet fundamentally it was a death that she had long desired, and it was at least painless and swift.

Empress Elisabeth embodied the spirit of the Viennese *fin de siècle* as no other individual. She refused to play the roles of wife, mother and empress, the representative figurehead of a huge empire, which tradition had thrust upon her. Instead she fought for what the feminist movement of the 20th century was to proclaim under the catchword of self-realisation. In her sensitivity, nervosity, her restlessness and lack of a real home, as well as in her egocentricity, she took the cult of the individual which was so typical for the times to extremes, and ultimately failed.

She worked consciously to create her legend for posterity, the legend of a hauntingly beautiful, misunderstood and deeply lonely Elisabeth, who refused to be merely an imperial figurehead. What remains is the myth.

Chronology
of the life of Empress Elisabeth
Robert Holzschuh

View of the Erechtheum on the Acropolis in Athens. The woman in black is possibly Empress Elisabeth. Elisabeth, Marie Valerie and her husband Franz Salvator visited Athens on March 23rd and 24th 1891.

It is hard to imagine a greater contrast. On the one hand there was Franz Joseph, who became emperor at the age of eighteen, and believed implicitly in his divine right to rule. He spent his whole reign attempting to save the monarchy, burying himself with industry and zeal, albeit without much imagination, in the never-ending deluge of official documents. On the other hand there was Elisabeth with her extravagantly emotional nature, who knew all too well that only a vagary of fate had led to her becoming empress at the tender age of sixteen. Elisabeth was determined to cast it off the imperial dignity that she had attained so easily and unexpectedly as fast and resolutely as she could. She turned her back on her imperial duties, in the fashion of one who would in any case have presented her subjects with their freedom long ago, had she possessed this power.

The imperial court and public life were unable to deprive her of one elementary right: the freedom to be different to the way that she was expected to be. In the memorable ultimatum she issued in Bad Ischl, dated August 27th 1865, Elisabeth succeeded in getting the emperor to agree to the following demand: »(...) I reserve the right to decide whatever pertains to my affairs, such as, inter alia, my choice of surroundings and place of residence.«

This, in a few words, sketches the route she took through life: she was not necessarily always present at those places and events where her presence was desired. She disliked the balls at court, avoided playing her part in the Corpus Christi processions,

Painting by Friedrich von Kaulbach of the empress, probably on Corfu, after 1898; pastel on paper (Museen des Mobiliendepots, Vienna).

Elisabeth during a stay at Karlsbad, June/July 1892, on the Hirschsprung mountain; newspaper wood engraving after a drawing by E. Limmer.

appeared neither at the opening of the new State Opera House nor at that of the Burgtheater. She was indifferent to the expectations and feelings of her subjects – the one thing an empress should never permit herself.

Elisabeth loved travelling and never wanted to stay in one place very long. She once remarked to her Greek tutor Christomanos: »If I should arrive somewhere and know that I could not depart from there ever again, even paradise would become a hell for me«.

Nonetheless, some of the prejudices held against her by her contemporaries prove to be untenable and exaggerated on closer inspection. The empress was often accused of spending too little time in the countries of the empire and in particular in Vienna. However, analysis of the dates of her travels astonishingly reveals that from her marriage onwards, she spent nearly three-quarters of her life in Austria and Hungary, and that she spent seventeen years, that is, nearly half this time, in Vienna. One further surprising fact also emerges: despite her position as crowned queen of Hungary, she was always reproached with favouring that country above all others in the monarchy. This accusation may also be regarded with scepticism, as she in fact only spent eight years of her life there altogether.

Much of Elisabeth's behaviour was resented – her travelling was frowned on, especially to the more exotic destinations. And yet if one considers the fact that the empress, who lived to the age of 60, spent scarcely eight years outside Austria-Hungary

Elisabeth, Emperor Franz Joseph and entourage on an excursion during their stay at Territet from the end of February to March 1893; print after a drawing by Wilhelm Gause.

and her native country of Bavaria, the situation begins to show itself in a new light. A further point to consider is that her journeys only seemed unexpected and aimless to many people because the empress, who generally planned her journeys well in advance, had not acquainted them with her plans. Alexander von Warsberg, who was entrusted with the empress's travelling plans, supposed in the autumn of 1885 that the empress would probably want to »spend a month at sea, without knowing where she was going or wanting to go anywhere in particular« (Letter to Count Lanckoronski of September 14th 1885). Unbeknownst to him, she had been pursuing a plan with her customary tenacity to become the first crowned head of Europe to visit Troy in order to view Schliemann's excavations.

Towards the end of her life, Elisabeth's journeys across Europe became more and more frequent. She longed more than ever for the warmth and light of the south, hoping that there her health would improve and her physical afflictions would be alleviated. From 1890 to 1898 she spent more than half her time away from Austria-Hungary, a circumstance facilitated by the improvements in transport and accommodation which were taking place at the end of the nineteenth century. Everywhere new railway lines and comfortable modern hotels were being built. The emperor for his part was pleased to place the elegant imperial yachts *Greif* and *Miramar* at his wife's disposal, for at this period he did not refuse any of his wife's wishes, as long as these were »fulfillable in practice and will not be too great an embarrassment to me«. The empress found travelling much easier and more convenient as she was no longer obliged to travel as court protocol had once demanded, with a retinue of more than fifty people. Although she had access to almost inexhaustible financial resources, she felt that a tenth of the customary number of accompanying staff would be quite sufficient to her needs.

Thus Elisabeth was often quite different to what people expected. »People do not know«, she once defended herself, »what to make of me, because I do not fit into any of their traditions or long-established notions. They do not want their pigeonhole categories disturbed.« People wrote of the empress that she roamed restlessly here and there, that she travelled as if possessed, driven by an inner disquiet. But one should not forget the long periods of quiet in which she found her inner peace. »Civilised people«, Elisabeth once remarked to her Greek tutor, »do not follow me into the wilderness – they probably have better things to do. Those are my long periods of solitude from which I realise that one feels the weight of one's existence most when one has contact with other people.«

After her assassination, Elisabeth's last journey was from Geneva to Vienna, where she was buried in the Kapuzinergruft (the crypt of the Church of the Capuchin Brothers) in accordance with Habsburg dynastic ceremonial. The empress had had a very different notion of what her last journey and funeral would be like. She had wanted to be buried on Corfu on the lonely mountain of Aya Kyriaki. »Here«, she consoled herself, »I will have only the stars above me, and the cypresses will utter sighs enough, more than people ever will: in their plaints I shall live more eternally than in the remembrance of my subjects.«

The course of Empress Elisabeth's life
(December 24th 1837–September 10th 1898)

Note: The vertical lines indicate a change of location. Whenever this involved a lengthy journey or if the exact date can no longer be established, dotted lines have been used. Short interruptions, excursions and detours are not included in the itinerary. Place names conform to modern usage.

Year	January	February	March	April	May	June
1853	Munich/Possenhofen					
1854	Munich/Possenhofen			Vienna	Vienna/Laxenburg	Moravia/Bohemia · Vienna
1855	Vienna				Vienna/Laxenburg	Possenhofen
1856	Vienna				Vienna/Laxenburg	
1857	Venice Verona Brescia	Milan	Mantua/Gorizia Ljubljana · Vienna		Budapest	Vienna/Laxenburg
1858	Vienna				Vienna/Laxenburg	
1859	Vienna				Vienna/Laxenburg	
1860	Vienna				Vienna/Laxenburg	
1861	Madeira				Spain/Corfu/Trieste	Vienna
1862	Venice				Reichenau on Rax	Bad Kissingen
1863	Vienna					Bad Kissingen
1864	Vienna					Bad Kissingen
1865	Vienna	Dresden	Vienna	Munich	Vienna	Ischl
1866	Vienna	Budapest		Vienna		Ischl
1867	Vienna	Munich · Zurich	Vienna		Budapest	Ischl
1868	Vienna		Budapest/Gödöllő			Ischl
1869	Vienna		Budapest/Gödöllő			Vienna
1870	Rome	Budapest/Gödöllő				Ischl
1871	Merano					Ischl
1872	Vienna	Merano		Budapest/ Gödöllő	Merano · Vienna	Ischl
1873	Vienna					

The colours denote:

Austria-Hungary
red: Vienna
red-white-red: Austria (excluding Vienna)
yellow: Hungary

Foreign countries
blue: Bavaria
white: other foreign countries

July	August	September	October	November	December	Year
Munich/Possenhofen	Ischl	Munich/Possenhofen				1853
Vienna/Laxenburg	Ischl	Vienna				1854
Vienna/Laxenburg	Ischl		Vienna			1855
Vienna/Laxenburg	Carinthia / Vienna	Ischl	Vienna	Trieste	Venice	1856
Vienna/Laxenburg	Ischl		Vienna			1857
Vienna/Laxenburg		Ischl	Vienna			1858
Vienna/Laxenburg/Reichenau on the Rax						1859
Vienna/Laxenburg	Possenhofen/Munich	Vienna		Journey to Madeira	Madeira	1860
Corfu				Venice		1861
Bad Kissingen	Possenhofen	Vienna/Reichenau on the Rax	Passau	Vienna		1862
Bad Kissingen		Vienna				1863
Bad Kissingen	Vienna	Vienna				1864
Bad Kissingen	Ischl		Vienna		Munich	1865
Vienna / Budapest		Budapest	Ischl	Vienna / Budapest	Vienna	1866
Ischl		Switzerland	Vienna			1867
Ischl	Lake Starnberg		Budapest/Gödöllő			1868
Garatshausen	Ischl		Budapest/Gödöllő		Rome	1869
Ischl	Neuberg (on the Mürz)		Merano			1870
Ischl/Lake Starnberg			Merano		Vienna	1871
Ischl		Possenhofen	Budapest/Gödöllő			1872
Vienna/Payerbach	Ischl	Vienna	Budapest/Gödöllő			1873

Year	January	February	March	April	May	June
1874	Munich	Vienna				
1875	Budapest/Gödöllő/Vienna				Ischl	
1876	Budapest Gödöllő / Munich	Budapest/Gödöllő	London/Towcester	Vienna		Ischl
1877	Budapest/Gödöllő	Vienna	Göding	Vienna		
1878	Cottesbrooke		Vienna			
1879	Vienna	Summerhill	Vienna	Budapest/Gödöllő		Ischl
1880	Vienna/Budapest/Gödöllő	Summerhill	Vienna	Budapest/Gödöllő		
1881	Vienna	Combermere	Vienna			Feldafing
1882	Vienna	Combermere	London	Vienna	Budapest/Gödöllő	Vienna	Feldafing
1883	Budapest/Gödöllő	Vienna	Baden-Baden	Munich	Vienna	Feldafing	Ischl
1884	Vienna		Wiesbaden/Heidelberg	Zaandvoort/Amsterdam	Feldafing/Munich
1885	Vienna	Vienna	Zaandvoort/Amsterdam	Heidelberg/Baden-Baden	Vienna	Feldafing/Regensburg
1886	Vienna	Miramare / Vienna	Baden-Baden	Budapest/Gödöllő	Vienna	Feldafing
1887	Vienna	Budapest	Salzburg	Mehadia	Mehadia/Sinai	Vienna	Ischl
1888	Vienna	Budapest/Gödöllő	London/Bournemouth	Baden-Baden/Munich	Vienna	Ischl
1889	Vienna	Budapest/Gödöllő	Ischl	Wiesbaden	Vienna
1890	Vienna	Budapest/Gödöllő	Wiesbaden/Heidelberg	Vienna	Vienna
1891	Vienna	Budapest/Gödöllő	Corfu/Athens	Sicily	Corfu	Vienna	Munich	Vienna
1892	Vienna	Miramare	Corfu	Vienna	Karlsbad
1893	Seville/Gibraltar/Balearics/Barcelona	French Riviera	Territet	Genoa/Naples	Corfu	Vienna
1894	Madeira	Gibraltar/Marseilles	Cap Martin	Lichtenegg/Vienna/Munich
1895	Algiers	Cap Martin	Corsica	Corfu	Vienna/Munich/Lichtenegg
1896	Cap Martin	Corfu	Budapest Gödöllő	Vienna	Vienna
1897	Biarritz	Cap Martin	Territet	Vienna	Bad Kissingen
1898	San Remo	Territet	Bad Kissingen	Bad Brückenau	Vienna

July	August	September	October	November	December	Year
Ischl	Isle of Wight/London	Baden-Baden / Possenhofen		Budapest/Gödöllő		1874
Ischl	Sassetôt		Paris / Munich / Vienna	Budapest/Gödöllő		1875
Feldafing	Ischl	Corfu/ Athens	Budapest/Gödöllő			1876
Vienna	Ischl	Feldafing	Budapest/Gödöllő			1877
Ischl		Tegernsee / Vienna	Budapest/Gödöllő			1878
Ischl	Munich Tegernsee	Ischl	Vi- enna	Budapest/Gödöllő		1879
Vienna	Ischl		Vienna/Budapest/Gödöllő			1880
Ischl			Budapest/Gödöllő/Vienna			1881
Ischl			Budapest/Gödöllő/Vienna			1882
Ischl		Mürz- steg	Budapest/Gödöllő/Vienna			1883
Ischl		Vienna	Budapest/Gödöllő	Vi- enna	Budapest/ Gödöllő	1884
Ischl/Gastein/ Zell am See		Ischl	Radmer	Corfu/Troy/ Egypt	Budapest/ Gödöllő	Budapest/ Gödöllő	1885
Ischl	Gastein	Ischl		Vi- enna	Budapest/ Gödöllő	Vienna	1886
Cromer	Kreuth	Ischl		Corfu/Ithaca	Budapest/ Gödöllő	Vi- enna	1887
Gastein	Ischl	Bavaria	Ischl	Vi- enna	Corfu/Levkás/ Missolonghi/Asia Minor	Vienna	1888
Ischl/ Feldafing	Gastein	Ischl	Cam- piglio	Meran	Corfu	Tu- nisia/ Malta	Vienna	Mira- mare	1889
Gastein	Felda- fing	I.o.Wight/ Paris	Bor- deaux/ Lisbon	Gibraltar/ Algeria/Corsica	Menton/ Florence/ Livorno	Naples	Corfu	Vienna	1890
Gastein	Felda- fing	Ischl	Corfu	Cairo	Vienna	1891
Karlsbad	Ischl	Zurich/Lu- cerne/Inter- laken	Budapest/ Gödöllő	Vienna/ Lichtenegg	Sicily/Mallorca/ Malaga/Granada	1892
Gastein	Ischl	Venice	Budapest/ Gödöllő	Vienna/ Lichtenegg	Algeria	1893
Madonna di Campiglio	Ischl	Corfu	Budapest/ Gödöllő	Vienna	Algeria	1894
Bartfeld	Ischl	Aix-les- Bains	Budapest/ Gödöllő	Vienna	Cap Martin	1895
Bavaria	Ischl	Vienna	Budapest/ Gödöllő	Vienna/ Lichtenegg	Biarritz	1896
Schwal- bach	Ischl	Karersee	Merano	Budapest/ Gödöllő	Vienna	Biarritz	Paris	1897
Ischl	Bad Nauheim	Caux/ Geneva				1898

Imperial living

Eva B. Ottillinger

The room known as the »Walnut Room« at Schönbrunn Palace; watercolour by Franz Heinrich, 1855/60 (k. k. Schlösser Artstetten und Luberegg).

The »Imperial Style«

Today's visitor to the imperial apartments of the Hofburg in Vienna and Innsbruck or the Hietzing tract of Schönbrunn Palace can form only a very fragmentary impression of the ambience in which Emperor Franz Joseph I (1830–1916) and Empress Elisabeth (1837–1898) lived, as all of the apartments on public display have a very uniform appearance. The furnishings consist of neo-Rococo furniture, mostly in white and gold with red damask upholstery, a material also used for the wall-hangings. This imperial style of furnishing had been created at the Viennese court in the generation preceding Franz Joseph, under Emperor Ferdinand I (ruled from 1835 to 1848).

After the death of Emperor Franz II (I) in March 1835, Ferdinand, his eldest son and heir, moved from his Crown Prince apartments in the Amalia tract of the Hofburg, which had been newly refurbished in 1831 on the occasion of his marriage to Maria Anna of Savoy, to the first floor of the Leopoldine tract, which today houses the presidential chancellery. This move was a conscious symbol of continuity on the imperial throne of Austria; the state rooms and the living quarters of the emperor now again formed a unit, as they had done in the days of Charles VI, Maria Theresa and Joseph II. The 18th-century interiors used by Franz II (I) only on ceremonial occasions had to be comprehensively restored and refurbished for Ferdinand I. This »improvement of the interior appointments«, as the *Obersthofmeister* (Master of the Emperor's

The »Paintings Room« of Archduchess Sophie in the Hofburg, Vienna; chromolithograph after a watercolour by Rudolf von Alt, 1855 (Museen des Mobiliendepots, Vienna).

Household; the highest office at court) wrote, »is to proceed from the principle of retaining the current style«, that is, of ensuring that the renovations matched the existing decorations and furnishing. The »Blondel style« (as the Rococo was known at that time) as the *Obersthofmeister* continued, was »appropriate to the decorum of the Supreme Imperial Court«.

The apartments occupied by Ferdinand and Maria Anna in the Hietzing tract of Schönbrunn Palace were refurnished with pieces in the Blondel style after 1835, with care being taken to match them with the existing wall-decorations dating from the time of Maria Theresa. In 1844 the court cabinet-maker Ernest Gissl made »by imperial command for the sitting-room of the Emperor […] new [pieces] with gilding and silk upholstery to match the room panelled in walnut and decorated with gilding, to replace the extremely threadbare existing furniture«. The new furnishings for this room, which was known as the »Walnut Room« on account of its walnut panelling, were recorded in a watercolour by Franz Heinrich dated 1855/60, and can still be seen today in the form in which they were commissioned by Ferdinand.

The apartments on the second floor of the Hofburg belonging to Archduke Franz Karl (1802–1878) and Archduchess Sophie (1805–1872), the parents of Emperor Franz Joseph, were of particular importance for the subsequent consolidation of the Blondel style. When a »picture room« was refurbished for the archduchess, the director of the imperial paintings gallery advised red as the most suitable background colour for the paintings. The Director of Court Furnishings duly ordered carmine silk damask for the wall-hangings, and the same fabric was used for the upholstery of the pieces of Blondel furniture »of carved wood in white and gold« personally chosen by Archduchess Sophie. A water-colour from 1855 by Rudolf von Alt records the furnishing and decoration of this room, which has not been preserved in its original state, showing the prototype of the »strawberry damask« which was to become so popular in the Franz Joseph era. The harmonious effect of the combination of white, red and gold became an important model for the style of the apartments furnished for Emperor Franz Joseph.

Thus a combination of the pious wish to preserve the interior decoration from the era of Maria Theresa, together with the need to legitimise the »Kindly« (in fact feeble-minded) monarch Ferdinand through the evocation of the history of the style consciously propagated by the court administration, resulted in what became known as the »Imperial Style«.

The apartments of Franz Joseph and Elisabeth

It was a Habsburg tradition that a new ruler or married couple should move into a new set of apartments that had been refurbished for them. It was not only the apartments in the Vienna Hofburg that were affected, but also those in the palaces at Schönbrunn and Laxenburg, which were regularly occupied by the whole court during the summer months.

During the course of the 1848 revolution, Emperor Ferdinand I had abdicated in favour of his nephew, Franz Joseph. The young monarch was to be the first Austrian emperor to reside in the Imperial Chancellery tract of the Hofburg which had lost its administrative function in 1806 with the dissolution of the Holy Roman Empire. Refurbishment in the Blondel style started. At first Franz Joseph had to move from the apartments he had occupied as Crown Prince on the second floor of the Schweizertrakt into the rooms of his predecessor in the Leopoldine tract. When the young monarch married Elisabeth, Duchess of Bavaria, the apartments in the Amalienburg, adjacent to the Imperial Chancellery tract, which had been occupied since 1835 by Archduchess Maria Anna and her *Obersthofmeisterin*, Countess Khevenhüller, were refurbished for the new empress. A team of craftsmen, including master cabinet-maker Heinrich Dübell, the upholsterer Josef Hassa, the sculptor Auguste La Vigne and the mirror and glass manufacturer Joseph Lobmeyr, refurbished a bedroom and a dressing room together with several salons and smaller rooms, whereby the Rococo decoration of the rooms was preserved and complemented by new furniture and decoration in the Blondel style. The couple was not able to move into the apartments until 1857.

At Schönbrunn Palace, Franz Joseph had moved into the apartments of his predecessor in the Hietzing tract after 1848. These were »set in order« for him but not totally refurbished. An apartment for Empress Elisabeth immediately adjacent to that of the emperor had been refurnished in 1854. The Blondel-style furnishings and decoration were executed by the glass and mirror manufacturer Lobmeyr, the master stove-maker Erndt, the gilders Köderl and Zentner, and the sculptor Anton Schröfel. The new furniture, such as the elaborately-carved rosewood suite for the bedroom, was made by the firm of Schwaigard and Abermann.

A new apartment was furnished for the imperial couple in the Blauer Hof at Laxenburg, another residence of the imperial family. The craftsmen involved here included the gilder Johann

The marital bedroom of Elisabeth and Franz Joseph in Schönbrunn Palace with the furniture made by Schwaigard und Abermann (1854); recent photograph.

Zentner, the master stove-maker Wilhelm Fressler and the upholsterers August Zenthner and Wilhelm Trögler; the carpets were supplied by Philipp Haas, the upholstery fabrics by A. C. Lechleitner and the new furniture was made by Philipp Schmidt.

Besides these apartments in regular use, the imperial couple had various quarters for use while travelling, such as the Salzburg Residenz or the Hofburg at Innsbruck. Since 1849, the former had been the permanent residence of Dowager Empress Caroline Auguste (1792–1873), the widow of Emperor Franz II (I). It was decided that the Wallis Rooms in the Residenz should be newly refurbished in the Blondel style for »royal guests«. The work was carried out from 1855 to 1861 by craftsmen from Vienna and Salzburg under the supervision of Carolina Auguste. The furniture was supplied by the Salzburg cabinet-maker Wessicken, while the upholstery was executed by Pfanzelter, also a native of the city. The mirrors were supplied by Lobmeyr from Vienna and the upholstery fabrics by the Vienna manufacturers Bujatti und Lechleitner's Erben.

The imperial apartments in the Hofburg at Innsbruck had been completely refurnished with pieces by the master cabinet-maker Johann Nepomuk Geyer in 1838, when Emperor Ferdinand I had stayed there on the way to his coronation as King of Lombardy and Venetia in Milan. Thus the refurbishment of these apartments for Franz Joseph and Elisabeth only started in 1857 and was not completed until 1866. The court sculptor August La Vigne, as interior decorator and entrepreneur, collaborated closely on this project with the *Obersthofmeister* in Vienna, who was in charge of the decoration of the apartments in the Blondel style as well as the execution of the furniture and interior decoration. Carpets and fabrics were supplied by Philipp Haas, mirrors and chandeliers by Lobmeyr.

The way the imperial apartments were decorated and furnished was chiefly decided by the Court Administration, which had a practised team of craftsmen and purveyors to the court at its disposal. The style of the furnishings was never a subject for debate: the Blondel style was »appropriate to the decorum of the Supreme Imperial Court«, and was to remain so until the end of the monarchy.

The imperial apartments as residence and museum

The decoration of the apartments occupied by the imperial family was not limited to the furnishings acquired by the Court Administration as imperial court property; in their private quarters they also had numerous family portraits, personal gifts and dedicational pieces, as well as individual items from the imperial art collections.

However, these features of the imperial family's private world vanished with the death of the occupants and the subsequent transformation of the apartments into state rooms on public display. A comparison of how they looked when they were still lived in and their present state illustrates the difference. Since the various places that Empress Elisabeth lived in will be described in detail in the following chapters, here the apartments occupied by Franz Joseph will be taken as an example.

»All the world would like to know what sort of surroundings the Emperor lives in«, it says in *Viribus Unitis*, the »Book of the Emperor« published in 1898. The information given is as follows: »The actual living quarters consist of a bedroom and a study, together with smaller reception rooms which connect with the apartments of the Empress […]. The Emperor's bedroom is only moderately wide, but very long, with just one window, and its uncommonly plain furnishing could almost be called »grandfatherly«. […] The study cum sitting-room is more sumptuously furnished […]. Here he spends almost all the waking hours which are not devoted to his ceremonial duties as monarch. […] The Emperor's writing-desk stands right by the window […]. Thick, dark carpets cover the floor of the study. Deep, soft easy-chairs in no particular order stand ready for the few select visitors whom the Emperor receives here.«

The contemporary description of the furnishings is illustrated by historic photographs of the study which were taken around 1880, before the Emperor's apartments were equipped with electric light in the 1890s. These photographs provide an authentic record of the furnishings of the room, including the neo-Rococo rosewood furniture made by the court cabinetmaker Heinrich Dübell. There are also several portraits: near his writing-desk the emperor had two very private portraits by Winterhalter of the young Elisabeth with her hair loose. A major difference to the appearance of the room today is the position of the furniture. As recorded in *Viribus Unitis*, the emperor's writing-desk stood by the light at the window, thus relieving the otherwise unbroken succession of identical double doors formed by the Baroque ground-plan of this tract of the Hofburg. Today the roped-off »corridor« for visitors has necessitated the writing desk being moved further back into the room.

There are also several paintings which record what the emperor's apartments at Schönbrunn Palace looked like while they were lived in, as well as a detailed description by one of his guards officers, Erwein Lobkowicz. The latter writes: »Some days after the burial of Emperor Franz Joseph, old Ketterl [the

Franz Joseph's study in the Vienna Hofburg, looking towards the emperor's bedroom, before electric lighting was installed in the palace; photograph by Stillfried, c./after 1880.

Franz Joseph's study in the Vienna Hofburg, looking towards the Konferenzzimmer, before electric lighting was installed in the palace; photograph by Stillfried, c./after 1880.

Franz Joseph's study in the Vienna Hofburg as it looks today, viewed from the windows; recent photograph.

Imperial living

emperor's valet de chambre] showed me the apartments of his late master at Schönbrunn. The first large study [known as the »Walnut Room«], a handsome room, all in white and gold, had quite decent furniture; the large Rococo bureau was a fine piece. [...] The second study was considerably plainer, furnished mainly with so-called »treasury« furniture. The writing-desk in particular was more than tasteless, a polished brown structure of the dreadful type of furniture produced in the Seventies. [...] The walls of this room and also of the bedroom as well as all the upholstery were covered with heavy, dark-brown silk which was decorated with an irregular pattern of ivy leaves in green; it looked old-fashioned and yet novel. [...] In the second bedroom the furniture was the same as in the second study. The bed, quite plain, of brown-painted metal, was shielded on both sides by folding cloth screens. Above it hung a yellowed bouquet of roses under glass, the flowers that Empress Elisabeth was carrying when she was murdered in Geneva. The fire screen consisted of three large frames containing numerous images of saints under glass; these were all from Frau Schratt, from various places of pilgrimage. The washstand was fairly modern, of brass and marble, the bedside cabinet and the wardrobes standing against the walls of the same kind as the writing-desk in the second study. It was furniture that one would no longer have seen in any better sort of household.«

The private study and bedroom of Franz Joseph were re-furnished in 1868 with furniture by the court cabinet-maker Heinrich Dübell. The furniture that Erwein Lobkowicz called »tasteless« in 1916 is still to be seen in both rooms.

A portrait of Franz Joseph dating from 1916 by Franz Matsch showing the monarch at his desk and a watercolour of the bed-room by Berthold Löffler, executed immediately after the death of the emperor, show these two rooms with all their private accessories. A comparison of the latter picture with another watercolour of the same room by Josef Kraal in 1922, painted after the end of the monarchy, demonstrates clearly the dif-ference between a room that is lived in and a room that is purely for display, without any personal touches.

This difference is far less evident in the case of rooms that were used for ceremonial or official purposes. If one compares Franz Heinrich's painting of the Walnut Room from 1855/60 and Josef Kraal's view of the same room from 1922, the interior decoration and furnishings seem more or less identical, with the exception of a single writing-desk. The Rococo bureau de-scribed by Lobkowicz – which was not yet part of the furnish-ings when Heinrich painted the room, and had gone by the time Kraal painted his – was a private possession of the emperor and had to be replaced after 1919 when Schönbrunn was turned into a museum.

When the rooms of the imperial palaces lost their function as living quarters with the end of the monarchy, their transform-ation into places on display to the public occurred in different ways. While the furnishings of the private quarters have only partially been preserved, without the everyday details and per-sonal touches, the character of the rooms used for ceremonial purposes has changed very little. In fact, the rooms used today

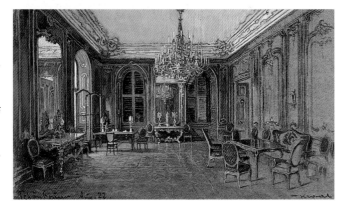

Above left: Emperor
Franz Joseph I in
his study at Schön-
brunn Palace; oil
painting by Franz
von Matsch, 1916
(Historical Museum
of the City of
Vienna).

Above right:
Emperor Franz
Joseph's bedroom
at Schönbrunn;
watercolour by
Berthold Löffler,
1916 (Museen des
Mobiliendepots,
Vienna).

Centre: Emperor
Franz Joseph's
bedroom at
Schönbrunn;
watercolour by
Josef Kraal, 1922/23
(Schloss Schön-
brunn Kultur- und
Betriebsges. m. b. H.).

Below: Emperor
Franz Joseph's
»Walnut Room« at
Schönbrunn Palace;
watercolour by
Josef Kraal, 1922/23
(Schloss Schön-
brunn Kultur- und
Betriebsges. m. b. H.).

for state banquets or the suite of the Federal President are still
furnished in the Blondel style, the neo-Rococo furnishings in
white and gold with their »strawberry-damask« upholstery, and
it is still the style which is associated with the official aspect of
the Republic of Austria on state occasions.

Residences

The Achilleion on Corfu; wood engraving after a drawing by R. Püttner.

Buda Palace, the presentation of the gifts in kind on June 10th 1867; wood engraving after a drawing by Franz Kollarz.

Gödöllő Palace; watercolour from the empress's private collection.

Schönbrunn Palace; gouache by G. Heisinger and M. Kolb.

The Blauer Hof at Laxenburg; copper engraving, 1838.

The Hermes Villa
in the game park at
Lainz; photograph,
c. 1889/99.

The Vienna Hofburg
looking towards the
Amalienburg and
the Imperial Chan-
cellery tract from the
inner palace court-
yard; drawing by
Rudolf von Alt, 1847.

The Imperial Villa
at Ischl; steel en-
graving, c. 1880/90.

Possenhofen Castle
on Lake Starnberg;
gouache, 1854.

The Palace of Duke
Max in Munich;
steel engraving,
c. 1840.

The Palace of Duke Max in Munich
– the birthplace of Elisabeth
Barbara Kuhn

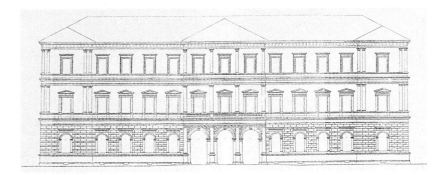

The palace in Munich's Ludwigstrasse, where Empress Elisabeth of Austria was born on December 24th 1837, was built during the course of the urban development of Munich at the beginning of the 19th century, when the city underwent huge expansion beyond the old city walls. One of the projects connected with this expansion was the Ludwigstrasse, which had been planned since 1816 to run northwards from the city centre. It originated in the wish of the then crown prince and later king, Ludwig I (1786–1868), to create a grand boulevard, whose façades were to be built in a uniform neo-Renaissance style. Two famous architects, Leo von Klenze (1784–1864) and Friedrich von Gärtner (1792–1847), translated the ideas of this potentate into concrete designs.

However, Ludwig was not willing to commit any of his own resources to realise his dream. He therefore sought wealthy backers for the project to build new residences which would conform to his architectural designs. He found one such backer at the end of 1827, albeit after considerable initial difficulties, in his future brother-in-law, Duke Maximilian of Bavaria (1808–1888), who married Ludwig's sister, Ludovika of Bavaria (1808–1892), in 1828.

The projected site was occupied by several houses. Following massive pressure from King Ludwig I, the city of Munich put up 131,000 gulden for the purchase of the necessary properties. Duke Maximilian contributed 50,000 gulden.

The ceremonial laying of the palace's foundation stone took place on April 28th 1828. The roof was on by November of the same year, but it was not until three years later, in October 1831, that the ducal family were able to move into their new home. It was inaugurated with a magnificent ball. The architect Leo von Klenze had built a palace in imitation of Italian city palaces in various styles of the Italian Renaissance, in particular those of the Roman and Florentine quattro- and cinquecento. On being entrusted with the commission, Klenze had stipulated that he was also to be in charge of the interior decoration. The building covered 0.563 hectares, with an additional 0.149 hectares for the garden courtyard, which from 1833 to 1844 housed the duke's famous circus.

The ground floor of the palace contained the duke's apartments, where his famous »Knights of the Round Table« used to meet. A secret staircase connected these rooms with the duchess's apartments directly above, where Empress Elisabeth was born. At the centre and in the right-hand section were ceremonial apartments,

Far left: the original front elevation of the palace of Duke Max by Leo Klenze from the year 1828, endorsed with a handwritten authorisation by King Ludwig I of Bavaria (private collection). The main façade was 63 m long, while the two side-wings of the horseshoe-shaped building extended over 43 m. This was adjoined to the west by a four-winged rear building. Leo von Klenze received the sum of 16,000 gulden as his architect's fee (worth approximately $ 260,000 in today's money).

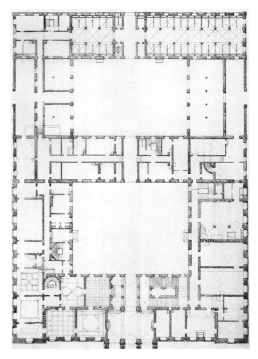

Ground plan of the ground floor, c. 1830 (Munich City Museum, Maillinger Collection). To the left of the main entrance were the duke's apartments. These were entered via the second door in the entrance archway through two anterooms. The outer rooms clockwise from the main entrance were: the First Salon, Second Salon, Pompeian Cabinet, study, bedroom, bathroom, cloakroom, library, secretary's room, archive. To the right of the main entrance were the stairs to the 1st and 2nd floors, the chapel, silver-room and utility rooms. The rear building contained stables, coach houses, servants' accommodation and the offices of the ducal administration. There were mezzanine floors above the ground floor of the main building as well as above the first floor.

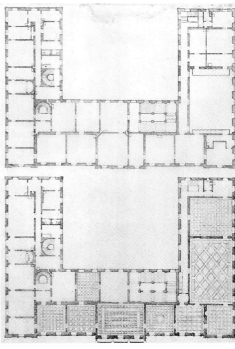

Below: ground plan of the first floor of the main building (Munich City Museum, Maillinger Collection). The outer rooms clockwise from top right were: the Yellow Salon/Grand Dining Room, ballroom, Pompeian Salon, games room or dining room, Mayer Room, reception room, the duchess's Green Salon, the duchess's Brown Salon, cabinet in Pompeian style, dressing-room, the duchess's bedroom with a secret staircase leading to the duke's apartments, bathroom, cloakroom, bedrooms for the younger children. The main staircase, the vestibule and the duchess's first and second anterooms were on the side facing the inner courtyard.

Above: ground plan of the 2nd floor: apartments of the older children, together with those of ducal household. Leo von Klenze had originally planned the same arrangement of rooms as on the first floor. Later plans show that the designs were altered to accommodate the needs of the ducal family; nearly every room could be entered from a corridor. It is not known when these alterations were carried out.

Above left: Duchess Ludovika's Green Salon; historical photograph. On the right-hand wall hung a portrait by Joseph Karl Stieler of Archduchess Sophie and her twin sister, Marie, Queen of Saxony. In the background to the left of the bust of King Maximilian I is a portrait of Empress Elisabeth of Austria. The furniture was white with gilt ornamentation. The walls had green silk hangings with an ornate gold pattern.

Above right: the Great Ballroom; historical photograph. Measuring 213 m², the ballroom was two storeys high. At the height of the second storey it was decorated with 16 frescoes by Wilhlem von Kaulbach (1804–1874) representing the myth of Cupid and Psyche. The ceiling was painted by Clemens Zimmermann. The Kaulbach frescoes were removed before the palace was demolished, and are today in the Collection of Music of the Bavarian State Library.

Below: reception room with monumental frescoes by Robert von Langer (1783–1846); historic photograph (private collection). The room extended over three window axes (8 x 13 m). To the left of the door leading to the private apartments of the duchess is the fresco »Allegory of Night«. The fresco to the right of the door represents Theseus after vanquishing the Minotaur; immediately to the right is Hercules leading Eurydice out of Hades after having subdued Cerberus. These frescoes were removed before the palace was demolished, but subsequently disappeared.

They were rediscovered by chance behind panelling in the Faculty of Law at Munich University in 1992.

Duchess Ludovika's bathroom; historical photograph. Klenze provided the apartments of both the duke and duchess with bathrooms. A copper bathtub originally stood between the two tiled stoves. The other occupants of the palace also had their own water closets and bathrooms.

Duke Max's theatre, looking towards the stage; historical photograph. The tent-like baldachin was striped in blue and white. Plays written by Duke Max were performed in the theatre. The exact location of the theatre in the palace is not known.

the size of which could be altered to fit the occasion. Eminent artists of the age decorated these rooms after designs by Leo von Klenze in the neo-Classicist style. Of particular interest are the Bacchus frieze by Ludwig von Schwanthaler (1802–1848) in the Yellow Salon, the cycle *Cupid and Psyche* by Wilhelm von Kaulbach (1804–1874) in the ballroom as well as the monumental frescoes of Greek mythology by Robert von Langer (1783–1846) in the reception room. The ceilings of the ducal couple's apartments and the ceremonial apartments were richly decorated with stucco work and frescoes. With both the architecture of the palace and its interiors, Klenze had created a *Gesamtkunstwerk*.

During the first few years the ducal couple held much-talked-about balls, parties, concerts and circus performances, and the family performed plays written by the duke in the small theatre.

The Yellow Salon with the 44 m bas-relief by Ludwig von Schwanthaler (1802–1848); historical photograph. The frieze depicts the myth of Bacchus. The walls of the room were faced with yellow stucco marble.

The frieze was removed before the palace was demolished and a large part of it was put up in the main banking hall of the Landeszentralbank im Freistaat Bayern.

Duchess Ludovika's dressing-room and bedroom; this photograph taken at the end of the 19th century reveals that the private apartments were altered over the course of the years. The painted stucco ceilings were subsequently covered by baldachin-like tapestry hangings.

Portraits of Empress Elisabeth and Queen Marie of Naples can be seen in the background. The connecting passageway led into the duchess's Pompeian Cabinet. The murals in this room can be made out in the background.

View of the interior of Duke Max's circus; pen-and-ink drawing by H. v. Mayer (Munich City Museum, Maillinger Collection). From 1833 to 1844 the circus was housed in the rear courtyard of the palace. It was a circular construction roofed with a marquee, and had wooden fittings as well as boxes and benches for the spectators. Initially the duke and duchess themselves showed off their riding skills in the ring.

The site of Duke Max's palace at No. 13, Ludwigstrasse in Munich is now occupied by the headquarters of the Landeszentralbank im Freistaat Bayern. Work began on the new building in 1938 but was brought to a halt by the Second World War. After the war it was completed by the architect Carl Sattler, who adapted the original designs from the National Socialist era.

However during the course of the years the ceremonial apartments came to be used only on rare occasions, the duke preferring his gentlemen's circles, held, among other places, in his *café chantant*, modelled on Parisian cafés, at the rear of the palace. One of the few festive high points in the middle of the 19th century was the ball held on December 28th 1853 to mark the forthcoming marriage of Duchess Elisabeth to Emperor Franz Joseph I of Austria. Elisabeth set off from the palace on April 20 1854 for her wedding in Vienna.

Not until the younger daughters of Duke Carl Theodor (1839–1909), Maximilian's successor, came of marriageable age at the end of the 19th century were the ceremonial apartments opened once more. The celebrations on the occasion of the duchesses' marriages brought all the old splendour back to this neo-Classical palace. No one could then have foreseen that it was to be the for the last time.

After the death of Carl Theodor in 1909, his son Ludwig Wilhelm (1884–1968) inherited the palace, but rarely lived there. In the years following the First World War, parts of the building were rented out for financial reasons.

The elegant neo-Classical building on one of Munich's most imposing streets was a thorn in the flesh to Adolf Hitler for whom it was not monumental enough. Duke Ludwig Wilhelm was forced to sell the property in 1937, and the site was earmarked for a main branch of the Reichsbank. On the centenary of Empress Elisabeth's birth scaffolding was put up around the palace, and in 1938 this neo-Classical jewel was demolished. Work began on the new building immediately, but was not completed (after altered designs) until after the Second World War. Since 1954 it has housed the headquarters of the Landeszentralbank im Freistaat Bayern.

Possenhofen Castle on Lake Starnberg
– the summer residence of the Dukes of Bavaria
Gerhard Schober

Possenhofen had been in the possession of the Dukes of Bavaria since the 16th century. One of the duke's chancellors, Jakob Rosenbusch, had a new manor house built which today still forms the core of the castle buildings. After a succession of different owners, it was bought back for the court at Munich in 1669 by the Prince Elector Ferdinand Maria, who intended to use it for his hunting parties on the lake.

In 1664 he had a magnificent ceremonial boat, named the *Bucentaur*, built by Venetian boat-builders. Thirty metres long, with painted decoration and gilded carvings, it was accompanied by a whole flotilla of colourful galleys, rowing boats and other boats bearing staff and field-kitchens, which made for different points on the shore, depending on the occasion. These included the stag hunts, famous throughout Europe, in the shallows near the shoreline, or afternoon coffee-parties held in colourful Turkish marquees, or evening banquets with music and elaborate firework displays.

Towards the end of the 17th century, Possenhofen came into the possession first of the Barons von Wampl, then of the Counts La Rosée. It was bought from them by Duke Max of Bavaria, the head of the collateral line of the Wittelsbachs, who had married Ludovika, the sister of King Ludwig I, in 1828. The purchase price of 145,000 gulden also included Garatshausen Castle.

Possenhofen had retained the appearance of a plain, late-Renaissance country house until 1834, despite several alterations. It consisted of a more or less square building with a pitched roof and towers at each corner, and was surrounded by a fortified wall. Duke Max first had this wall pulled down and the interior of the building extensively refurbished. A large part of the Renaissance and Baroque furnishings was removed, such as the dark, heavy ceilings from the 16th century, the huge tiled stoves and four-poster beds, the old chapel on the ground floor, as well as much furniture that had survived over the centuries. The rooms were fitted out according to contemporary taste and furnished accordingly, either in elegant neo-Classical or the plainer Biedermeier style. A new double staircase was installed. The alterations to the exterior of the building, however, were more restrained. The windows were moderately enlarged and equipped with green shutters, as was usual in that part of the country, and wrought-iron balconies were added to a number of rooms.

The most radical alteration was the addition of a horseshoe-shaped wing in place of the old Baroque outhouses. This new building, which was

much larger than the old house itself, was linked to the west front of the house by the chapel. It served as accommodation for visitors, residential quarters for the royal household and the servants, and also contained stabling and coach-houses. It was probably designed by Daniel Ohlmüller, a pupil of Klenze, who is documented as the architect of the new chapel which was built at the same time.

The overgrown former game reserve was transformed into a park on the English model. Karl von Leoprechting, a local historian who saw the park at this time, gives an enthusiastic description of the smooth expanses of

Possenhofen Castle on Lake Starnberg

Above left: drawing allegedly made by Sisi of Possenhofen, which was called »Possi« by the family (location according to C. Conti's »Schloss Wallsee«, 1940).

Below left: Elisabeth at the time of her betrothal in front of Possenhofen Castle; steel engraving by Andreas Fleischmann after a painting by Karl Piloty and Franz Adam, 1853. The painting was formerly owned by Emperor Franz Joseph (now in the Thurn und Taxis Collection, Regensburg).

Possenhofen Castle, main façade with the chapel, dated August 18th [18]54; washed ink drawing by an anonymous artist (Munich City Museum).

grass and the majestic groups of trees. The swept gravel paths were lined with flower beds, lilac bushes and rhododendrons. Rides were cut through the woods affording impressive views of the lake and the Alps beyond it. Duke Max had without doubt created the most beautiful gardens on Lake Starnberg.

Possenhofen remained the family's favourite summer residence until 1920. Elisabeth, the future empress of Austria, (who was not born here, as is often asserted) spent the holidays of her youth here. Her memories of that happy, carefree time were so strong that as empress she returned every summer for a few weeks. With due regard for imperial etiquette, she did not reside at Possenhofen but in Feldafing, at the Strauch Hotel, later to be renamed the Empress Elisabeth Hotel. Her brothers and sisters also spent the best times of their youth here, her brothers Carl Theodor, Ludwig Wilhelm and Max Emanuel, her sisters Helene, later to wed the Prince of Thurn und Taxis, Marie, who married the future King Francis II of The Two Sicilies, and Sophie, who was briefly married to Ludwig II and later became the wife of the Duke of Alençon.

ELISABETH
Kaiserin von Oesterreich

Elisabeth with Possenhofen in the background; lithograph by H. Kohler after a photograph, 1853.

Façade and interior of the chapel designed by Daniel Ohlmüller, one of von Klenze's pupils; watercolour by Carl Roesner, professor at the Academy of Fine Arts, Vienna. 1854 (Schloss Schönbrunn Kultur-und Betriebsges. m. b. H.)

Äussere Ansicht der Schlosskapelle.

Innere Ansicht der Schlosskapelle.

Possenhofen Castle after renovation and conversion into owner-occupied flats in the 1980s (photograph taken in 1985).

The stairwell of the castle (in 1985); the double staircase is one of the few remaining features from the time of Duke Max).

Elisabeth, the daughter of Duke Carl Theodor and future Queen of Belgium, was born here at Possenhofen in 1876.

When Duke Max died in 1888, his son, Duke Carl Theodor, who became a famous eye specialist, took over possession of the estate. In 1909 Duke Ludwig Wilhelm inherited Possenhofen and lived there until 1920. From then until the outbreak of the Second World War it was a rest home for disadvantaged children from Munich. During the war it was a field hospital. At the end of the war Possenhofen came into the possession of the State of Bavaria, and in 1951 the Rex factory for auxiliary bicycle engines was set up here. The building itself had become increasingly dilapidated, and in 1982, after the factory had closed down, it was sold and converted into owner-occupied flats. While the interior was completely altered, the façade was restored to something approximating its historic appearance.

When the Italian film director Luchino Visconti came to Lake Starnberg to make his film about Ludwig II, great times seemed to have returned to Possenhofen. However, with the aid of mock neo-Gothic additions made of polystyrene, it was transformed into Ludwig's Berg Castle, as the director had been refused permission to film there. Obviously the interior could no longer be used for the film. Even

the park had lost much of its beauty; most of it was purchased by the City of Munich in 1963 and made into a public bathing and recreational area.

The Vienna Hofburg
– the official residence of Empress Elisabeth

Georg J. Kugler

On April 23rd 1854 Princess Elisabeth made her ceremonial entry into Vienna as the bride of the emperor. She had spent the night following her arrival at Schönbrunn and the next morning she drove in a six-horse carriage to the Theresianum, and from there continued her journey across the Karlsplatz to the Hofburg in a gilded gala carriage – drawn by eight horses, the exclusive privilege of an empress – once used by Napoleon at his coronation in Milan.

The next day she was married to the emperor in the Augustinerkirche (Church of the Augustine Brethren). The wedding was followed by an alarming number of festivities, official receptions and audiences, as well as family luncheons and dinners which were always accompanied by the censorious criticisms of her new mother-in-law. In short, Elisabeth was plunged into the overpowering world of the imperial

Hofburg and there took up residence. It was to remain her main official residence for the rest of her life, but she disliked the Hofburg and stayed away from it whenever she could.

There were three very understandable reasons for her dislike. After only a few days it became obvious to her that she had completely lost her youthful independence and that her poetic sense of freedom would very soon be stifled.

Elisabeth was nominally the empress, but the Hofburg was in fact ruled by her overbearing and tactless mother-in-law and aunt, Archduchess Sophie. She took it upon herself to »educate« the sixteen-year-old wife of her son, whom she idolised, and was later to summarily take charge of the upbringing of Elisabeth's own children.

At the Hofburg, her husband the emperor was completely occupied

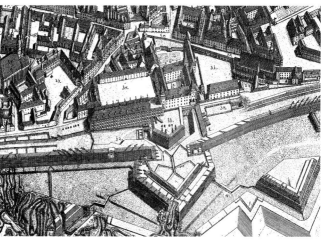

Far left: the façade of the Imperial Chancellery tract facing the inner palace courtyard was built after designs by Joseph Emanuel Fischer von Erlach between 1726 and 1730, while the tract facing Schauflergasse had been begun in 1723 after designs by Johann Lucas von Hildebrandt. The Imperial Chancellery was the central authority of the Holy Roman Empire of the German Nation until its dissolution in 1806.

This view of the inner palace courtyard is from the »Topographia Austriae inferioris« by Georg Matthaeus Vischer (1672). To the left is the Schweizertrakt with its medieval towers which adjoins the Leopoldine tract (1660–1666) that had recently been completed. To the right is the Amalienburg, built for the future emperor Rudolf II between 1575 and 1583. The exterior of the Amalienburg has remained essentially unchanged since it was built. The rooms on the main floor facing the courtyard were later to be occupied by Elisabeth.

The Hofburg from a bird's-eye view of Vienna by Daniel Suttinger executed at the time of the second Turkish siege in 1683 (Historical Museum of the City of Vienna). The palace adjoined private citzens' houses and monastery buildings on the city side and was bound by the city walls and defences to the south-west. Of the buildings still standing today, only the Schweizertrakt, the Leopoldine tract and the Amalienburg existed at this time. They enclosed the inner palace courtyard which had formerly been a tiltyard. To the east, a short distance away, was the Stallburg. At that time the Hofburg did not have a main façade as such.

with affairs of state both important and petty, as well as with the bureaucratic daily routine of his ministries, and was also exposed to the influence of his court officials and court society as a whole, which displayed a rare accord in its criticism and calumny of the young empress.

Elisabeth thus avoided the Hofburg and the people who dominated its rigid protocol. She lived elsewhere, travelling extensively, until the Compromise with Hungary in 1867, a cause she had championed and pleaded for with the emperor using the whole force of her bewitching personal charm. After this time she spent more than six months of every year as the crowned queen of Hungary at the palace in Buda/Ofen or at Gödöllő Palace.

To return to the beginning, however: before Elisabeth had had a proper chance to accustom herself

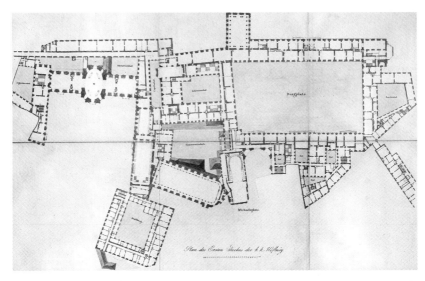

Ground plan of the main floor (1st floor) of the Hofburg (1st half of the 19th century). On the northwest side is the Amalienburg; the rooms facing the inner palace courtyard were occupied by the empress. To the north-east is the Imperial Chancellery tract which contained Emperor Franz Joseph's apartments, also facing the courtyard.

The Imperial Forum project; the first set of designs by Gottfried Semper and Carl Hasenauer, Zurich 1869. According to these plans, a throne room was to be built providing

the Hofburg with a main façade towards the Ringstrasse. To the side of the throne room two wings were projected which were to be linked to the new museums across the Ringstrasse by triumphal arches. Only the two museums (today the Kunsthistorische and the Museum of Natural History) and the south-east wing of the palace, known as the Neue Burg, were actually built. The latter today houses a part of the National Library. The throne room and the second wing of the palace were never built.

to the Hofburg, the young couple removed to Laxenburg in May 1854. From there Franz Joseph travelled daily into Vienna to attend to the affairs of state, leaving Elisabeth on her own. It was at Laxenburg, two weeks after the wedding, that she wrote the »long poem, whose significance should not be overestimated, owing its origin to a momentary mood of dejection, but which demonstrates that the character of this young girl, henceforth raised to the rank of empress, was no simple, ordinary one, but one that tended to outbursts of emotion which could seriously jeopardise her relationships with the world around her« (Conte Corti). Brigitte Hamann deals

One of the traditional ceremonies at the Viennese court was the Foot Washing on Holy Thursday performed by the emperor and empress for 12 elderly men and women. Since Elisabeth mostly chose to absent herself from the ceremony, the aged women had to make do with a gift of alms; wood engraving after a drawing by Vinzenz Katzler, 1870.

Court ball in the Hall of Ceremonies at the Hofburg, held in 1886. On the extreme left sit Empress Elisabeth and Crown Princess Stephanie, while guests are presented to them. To the right of them is Crown Prince Rudolf standing on his own. In the centre the emperor is engaged in conversation; after a drawing by Wilhelm Gause.

Empress Elisabeth descending the Schwarze Adler Staircase to greet Crown Prince Wilhelm of Prussia (October 20th 1869). This staircase was also used by Elisabeth to enter her apartments; after a drawing by J. Franz Kollarz.

with this poem at greater length in her essay (q.v. p. 15). Here it will be sufficient to repeat the second stanza:

I have awoken in a dungeon
With fetters on my wrists.
My longing grows ever stronger –
And Freedom! thou, turned away
from me!

Here we have the words »I have awoken in a dungeon«, a reference to the Hofburg which Elisabeth makes even more explicit in a later poem, entitled *Liberty*, from her *Winterlieder* (Songs of Winter) cycle. In the latter poem she writes of having a ship built, from whose mast the ensign of freedom will fly and on which she would escape

The Grand Salon of the empress; photograph, c. 1898/99. Taken shortly after the empress's death, this series of photographs represents something of a rarity, as the empress did not wish her apartments to be photographed.

The Small Salon of the empress; photograph, c. 1898/99.

The empress's dressing-room, which was also her exercise room: photograph, c. 1898/99.

from courtly life. In vain would she be sought upon the »far, high seas«:

Just try, oh you telegraphs,
To entrap me for a court ball
Back to the dungeon fortress;
Cast your nets in clear waters,
cast them in turbid waters,
Catch the seagull at will;
Hurrah! We've flown the nest, we're free!

This poem thus clearly allows the identification of the Hofburg with Elisabeth's »dungeon fortress«. But what exactly did Elisabeth mean by the word »dungeon«? The Hofburg, the imperial court, the Habsburg dynasty, or perhaps her marriage? At all events, she was facing the exact antithesis to the freedom of her childhood and youth. She was homesick, even when she was at Laxenburg, and begged the emperor only a few weeks after the wedding to be allowed to go to Ischl as soon as possible and to invite her mother and sister to visit her there.

Where did Franz Joseph and Elisabeth live in the Hofburg?

As crown prince, Franz Joseph had had apartments on the second floor of the Schweizertrakt, the oldest part of the palace. Following the turbulent events of autumn 1848, when Emperor Ferdinand signed his abdication at Olmütz and the eighteen-year-old Franz Joseph succeeded his uncle on the throne, questions such as which apartments would be most suitable for the new monarch were not of pressing importance. Franz Joseph did not return from Moravia to Vienna with his court until May 1859 and initially took up residence at Schönbrunn. Meanwhile Emperor Ferdinand vacated his apartments in the Hofburg and moved to Prague, where he henceforth resided at the Tuscan Palace on the Hradschin/Hradčany. Franz Joseph moved from the Schweizerhof to the Leopoldine tract at some point, probably occupying the apartments of his predecessor, which had been renovated as recently as 1831. However, this was only a temporary solution. It was certain right from the

beginning that following the tradition of the dynasty, the new ruler would move into new apartments, not those of his predecessor. The part of the palace which seemed most suitable was the Imperial Chancellery tract, which had lost its original function with the end of the Holy Roman Empire in 1806 and since that time had been occupied by various members of the imperial family. Archduke Johann, for example, had lived on the second floor whenever he visited Vienna, while the apartments on the east side of the main floor were occupied by the Duke of Reichstadt (Napoleon's son) until his early death in 1832, and later by Archduke Stephan, the Palatine of Hungary, whenever he made one of his increasingly rare visits to Vienna. The apartments still bear his name.

The apartments to the west of the Emperor's Staircase were now renovated for the new monarch, probably also in view of his forthcoming marriage, as hardly had his betrothal to Elisabeth taken place in 1853 when work started on adapting the rooms adjoining the Imperial Chancellery tract on the main floor of the Amalienburg for the young empress. The beautiful original decoration and furnishings from the 18th century were retained as exemplifying the grandeur appropriate to the dynasty, but were renovated and partly refurbished, with most of the furniture replaced with new pieces in the neo-Rococo style known in Vienna as the Blondel style. Objects from the imperial collections and palaces were also chosen to complement the furnishings. It seems that the emperor and empress did not finally move into these apartments until the end of 1857, as Franz Joseph wrote to his mother on November 13th 1857:

»We have decided to move into new apartments, since the ones we have lived in until now constantly evoke sad memories for Sisi [probably of her first daughter, Sophie, who had died on May 29th 1857, albeit in Budapest] and were very cramped. We shall

Emperor Franz Joseph's study in the Imperial Chancellery tract; photograph by Stillfried, c./after 1880. Facing the writing-desk is the portrait of Elisabeth wearing her hair loose and crossed over her breast. The oval painting is signed »F[ranz Xaver] Winterhalter Schönbrunn 1864« and is still today in the private possession of the Habsburg family. On the writing-desk stand photographs of the emperor's grandchildren.

Right: the Empress Elisabeth Memorial Room in the Small Salon; photograph, c. 1943; at that time several original documents pertaining to the empress were on display which are now preserved in the Austrian State Archives.

now be excellently accommodated and hope to move in within a few days, when the most necessary work has been completed. Sisi will have the Amalienhof Apartments and can use the Alexander Rooms for receptions and dinners. I will live [in the rooms extending] from the corner of the Imperial Chancellery to that horrible great room in which I shall hold my audiences. I am getting far too many rooms and do not intend to use all of them, a part of them including the Great Hall I even intend turning over to visitors when they are required. The little one will have the rooms that Uncle Johann used on his visits, in the Imper-

ial Chancellery above my future rooms. A staircase will be raised from the corner room of the Imperial Chancellery, so that Sisi can go to the little one directly from her rooms without having to go through an intervening room.«

The last sentence reveals only obliquely that this move had been preceded by Elisabeth's long struggle against her mother-in-law concerning the upbringing of her daughter Gisela. Gisela was the couple's second daughter, born on July 15th 1856. Only six weeks later, on August 30th, Franz Joseph wrote to his mother at Elisabeth's urging that the children be moved onto the same floor as the empress's rooms, and ordered the Radetzky Rooms on the main floor of the Schweizerhof to be prepared for them. It was characteristic for the unchallenged position that Franz Joseph's mother enjoyed that the nursery of the little Archduchesses Sophie and Gisela was not situated near their mother's apartments but one floor above, next to those of their grandmother. Elisabeth thus seldom went up there, as this meant that she also had to enter her mother-in-law's apartments.

The letter fell like a bombshell, as Franz Joseph had obviously expected,

for immediately afterwards he set off for Styria and Carinthia together with Elisabeth and in the middle of November the emperor and empress departed on a journey of several months to the southern regions of the empire. Via Laibach (Lubljana) and Trieste they went first to Venice. Their two daughters Sophie and Gisela were taken there to join their parents and stayed in the city over Christmas and New Year. During the first two months of 1857 Franz Joseph and Elisabeth stayed in Milan (without their children), returning to Vienna via Carniola in March. On May 4th the imperial family set off on a journey to Hungary, but little Sophie fell ill and died at Ofen (Budapest). Elisabeth returned to Vienna and Laxenburg while the emperor continued on his journey through Hungary. In the late autumn of 1857 the emperor and empress finally moved into their new apartments: Franz Joseph's in the Imperial Chancellery tract and Elisabeth's in the Amalia tract.

Elisabeth's apartments consisted of the marital bedchamber, a dressing-room which also served as an exercise room, a smaller room behind that, which was fitted up as a bathroom in

1876, a large (blue) salon, a study and a large and a small anteroom. The latter room, in which a guard was posted, led out onto the staircase known as the Schwarze Adlerstiege. Thus Elisabeth used these stairs to gain access to her apartments; that is, the sequence of the rooms was the exact opposite to that now followed by visitors to the state apartments.

Refurbished by a team of skilled court craftsmen, these rooms did not remain as they were in 1857. Apart from the works of art and objects that the empress was given as gifts, as well as pieces of furniture and carpets that she had brought here to replace others that had previously furnished these apartments, the wall-hangings, curtains and upholstery and even the tiled stoves were refurbished at regular intervals. As early as 1858 white silk wall-hangings and carpets were ordered for the »Blue Salon«, and the room was henceforward known as the »White Salon«. The study later became the Yel-low Salon or the Damask Room. These two rooms are today hung in red and known as the Large and Small Salons of the Empress. From around 1870 the marital bedroom was used by Elisabeth alone and she had her bed set up in this three-windowed room, behind a folding screen. This gave a more lived-in atmosphere to the large, bright room with its mirrors, by interrupting the otherwise unbroken succession of double doors. Her bed, which was a modern »healthy« iron bed, could be put away during the day. All of these rooms are today decorated in the classic combination of white, gold and red, although this was not carried out until a later date. The parquet flooring was laid with large or fitted carpets covered with oriental rugs belonging to Elisabeth which, like all the other personal pictures, furniture and articles, are no longer present. The rooms as the public sees them today bear little relation to the way they looked when the empress

One of the rooms in the Hofburg occupied by Ida von Ferenczy, the empress's confidante; photograph, c. 1906/07. The address of her apartments was Ballhaus *platz No. 6, 2nd floor, i.e., directly adjacent to those of the empress. Elisabeth used these rooms for secret meetings, but they were also used by Franz Joseph for his* *rendezvous with Katharina Schratt. The life-size statue of Elisabeth by Hermann Klotz (1906) was donated by Ida von Ferenczy to the Queen Elisabeth* *Memorial Museum in Budapest in 1907. This statue is thus not identical with the one today on display in the Hofburg, which is said to have been given* *by Franz Salvator, the husband of Marie Valerie.*

The Empress Elisabeth Memorial Room in the Small Salon, as it has looked since c. 1990. Today it contains fewer objects commemorating the empress than formerly.

His Majesty's personal kitchen; historical photograph. Besides the huge imperial-royal kitchens in the Schweizertrakt of the palace, there were also smaller kitchens in other parts of the palace where small meals could be prepared quickly. Empress Elisabeth's kitchen in the Amalienburg was supervised by Teresia Teufel, the only female chef at the Hofburg.

occupied them. This is documented by photographs taken of them and of her apartments at the Hermes Villa soon after Elisabeth's death.

The adjoining Alexander Apartments, which Elisabeth used for »receptions and dinners« as the emperor wrote, were renovated between 1883 to 1889 and the eleven windows were hung with new curtains.

The Elisabeth Apartments and the Alexander Apartments were occupied by Emperor Karl between 1916 and 1918. He too seldom lived at the Hofburg, spending most of his time at army headquarters in Baden or at the front.

After the collapse of the monarchy and the expropriation of imperial property, the imperial apartments were altered and furnished so that they could be put on display to the public. In the early 1930s the Small Salon was adapted as a memorial room to Empress Elisabeth. The life-size statue of the empress by Hermann Klotz in the salon was probably set up at that time. Archduke Franz Salvator is alleged to have donated it to the Republic of Austria for the express purpose of setting up an Empress Elisabeth Memorial Room.

The »Blauer Hof« at Laxenburg
– sojourns in the country during the early years of the imperial couple's marriage

Elisabeth Springer

The old moated castle at Laxenburg, an imaginary depiction from a Babenberg genealogy. In the foreground Duke Heinrich the Younger of Mödling is portrayed hawking, thus emphasising Laxenburg's position as the hunting lodge of the sovereign prince; roundel No. 22 of the Babenberg Genealogy, 1489–1493 (Klosterneuburg Monastery)

The *Kayserliche Hof- und Ehren-Calender* (Imperial Court Almanach) by Johann Jacob Koll for the year 1720 is prefaced by an interesting chronology. Here it records among other facts: »from the beginning and the initial foundation of the city of Vienna, more than 3,000 years; from the building of the Cathedral 380 and of the Great Tower 320 years; from the building of the first imperial fortress 508 years; from the building of Laxenburg Castle 328 years.«

This clearly indicates the importance of Laxenburg Palace for the imperial court. The beginnings of the site can be traced back to the 12th and 13th centuries. It consisted then of a moated castle with a farmstead, mill and other working buildings together with a large adjacent pasture-ground used for the oxen-market, held here up to the 16th century. However, its economic significance waned as it increasingly became a place of recreation.

It had been a royal hunting lodge possibly since the times of the Babenbergs, and certainly since the early Habsburg rulers, who acquired the property in 1306. Albrecht III was especially fond of the place, and had the castle rebuilt and decorated with statues from the old fortress on the Leopoldsberg above Vienna. He also had pleasure gardens and a game reserve laid out.

After periods in which Laxenburg suffered extensive damage in the wake of various armed conflicts, it began its steady rise from the 17th century onwards. From the reign of Leopold I,

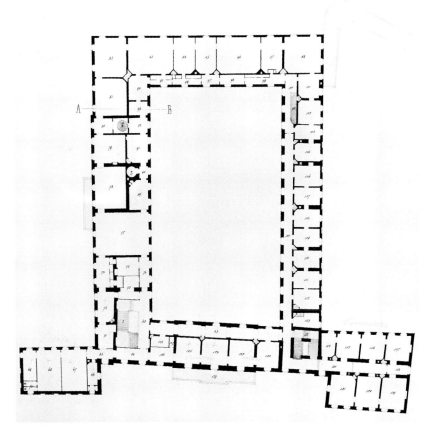

Ground plan of 1st floor of the Blauer Hof. The plan is drawn with the main entrance and the balcony above it facing the bottom of the page. Emperor Franz Joseph's apartments extended from the middle of the rear tract to the right-hand corner of the side tract. The empress's apartments lay to the left of these and also extended around the corner of the side tract as far as the spiral staircase. The rooms of both emperor and empress thus faced the garden with views of the surrounding park.

The imperial family watching military manoeuvres, 1771; painting by Franz Neuhauser (Schwarzenberg Palace, Vienna).

In the foreground is Maria Theresa dressed in mourning and surrounded by her children. On the left of the background is the old castle as it looked from c. 1755; on the right adjoining the castle are the buildings designed by Nikolaus Pacassi: the theatre, the dining tract and the Blauer Hof.

annual court residence at Laxenburg became the rule. This set off a building boom, which continued under Charles VI and Maria Theresa, as the nobility followed imperial example and built themselves castles of their own together with outbuildings.

The main attraction of Laxenburg, however, was the large park, which was newly laid out at intervals according to whatever fashion prevailed at that particular time. Emperor Franz II (I), who preferred Laxenburg above all other places, had the large lake and the Franzensburg built, an additional attraction which was shown to all foreign visitors.

From approximately 1760 onwards, the imperial family had always resided in the Blauer Hof (Blue Court). For Franz Joseph's parents, who married in 1824, apartments were refurbished in the latest style; however, after Emperor Franz's death, the court visits to Laxenburg became rare, with the result that the Blauer Hof remained empty.

Probably remembering the stays in the country from his childhood which are documented in numerous descriptions, Franz Joseph decided to reinstate these annual periods of summer residence at Laxenburg.

However, it was not until 1854 that the necessary alterations in the apart-ments of the future empress were discussed. This included renovating the floors, wall-hangings and walls, together with regilding work, the overhauling of the tiled stoves, as well as the making and upholstering of new furniture. For the numerous wedding guests, some of whom were to be accommodated at Laxenburg, rooms had to be made ready and thus the other buildings belonging to the palace also had to be renovated and furnished. Alterations were also undertaken in much of the park, and all the boats on the lake overhauled.

After the wedding on April 24th 1854 and all the audiences, receptions of deputations from the provinces, court balls and gala theatre perfor-mances, the imperial couple removed to Laxenburg on May 11th: »At a quar-ter to six o'clock Their Imperial-Royal Majesties proceeded by means of a special train to Laxenburg, thus com-mencing the royal sojourn in the country, for which every preparation had been made«. The Laxenburg *séjour*, as these stays were known, did not officially end until July 27th, al-though Franz Joseph and Elisabeth made a visit to Bohemia in the first half of June.

During the subsequent years the imperial couple also spent longer

Cavalcade with Emperor Joseph II in front of the Blauer Hof shortly after its comple- *tion; etching by Anton Ziegler after the drawing by Laurenz Janscha, 1786.* *Far right: views of the façades of the Blauer Hof from the courtyard and the garden respectively,* *from Franz Carl Wiedmann's »Neues Panorama von Wien [...] und Umgebung«;* *coloured copper engraving, 1838.*

The Blauer Hof at Laxenburg

Ansicht des K.K. Lustschlosses Laxenburg, von vorne.

54.

Prixner sc.

Wien, bey R. Sammer, Buchhändler beym Kärntherthore.

Laxenburg, von der Gartenseite.

457.

Prixner sc.

Wien, bey R. Sammer, Buchhändler beym Kärntherthore.

The Grand Staircase of the Blauer Hof; historical photograph, before/c. 1924.

The empress's salon; historical photograph, before/c. 1924. None of the rooms of the Blauer Hof still has its original furniture, as all fittings and furniture were removed to the safe-keeping of various Viennese museums when the castle was requisitioned by the German army during the Second World War.

Elisabeth, Franz Joseph and Crown Prince Rudolf and his wife, Stephanie, in the park at Laxenburg; painting by Karl Schwendinger the Elder, 1887 (Historical Museum of the City of Vienna). In the background is the Franzensburg, built by Emperor Franz II (I). This was not a residential building but a »summer house in the form of a Gothic castle«.

Exterior of the Blauer Hof seen from the courtyard; recent photograph.

periods at Laxenburg. In 1856 Elisabeth gave birth to her daughter Gisela at Laxenburg (Sophie, the first child, had been born in Vienna). The ceremonial baptism took place at Laxenburg in the large dining-room on the ground floor. The official record of this occasion contains the notable remark that the christening would only be carried out with »limited ceremony«, »since the *séjour* at Laxenburg is a sojourn in the country in the truest sense of the word, during which established court ceremonial is not used«.

In 1857, Elisabeth's mother and three sisters paid a visit of over three weeks to Laxenburg during which they resided in the old castle. During the *séjour* at Laxenburg in the year 1858, from May 15th to October 2nd, Crown Prince Rudolf was born and baptised, the ceremony taking place as in his sister's case with »limited ceremony« in the dining-room, which was festively decorated for the occasion.

In 1859 a different situation arose due to the military campaign in Lombardy. While Franz Joseph travelled to join his army, Elisabeth stayed at Laxenburg. She had a field hospital set up in the so-called Grünne House, one of the outbuildings of the castle, for the large numbers of wounded soldiers.

In 1860 the imperial family also started its country *séjour* at Laxenburg; however, in July Elisabeth suddenly departed for Possenhofen. In late autumn she began her journey

to Madeira, which was followed by visits to various spa resorts. In later years the empress stayed only briefly at Laxenburg.

In Franz Joseph's era, there were a total of 35 different buildings which were under the charge of the imperial-royal court administration. These buildings are today variously used, and in addition to those that are on display to the public, contain businesses, offices, flats and research institutions.

Schönbrunn Palace, the imperial summer residence

Elfriede Iby

Façade of Schönbrunn Palace with the Parade Court. The wing to the right on the west side of the Parade Court was occupied by the empress's youngest daughter, Marie Valerie, and is still known today by her name.

Plan of the »imperial-royal park of Schönbrunn«, 1908; coloured lithograph by Ofner, 1908. Under Maria Theresa the park was enlarged to its present dimensions of 1.2 km². The main palace building was occupied by the imperial family and the highest-ranking members of the imperial household. Court servants lived in the extensive outbuildings which also housed the court offices, some of which are still evident from their names, such as the Court Kitchens tract, the Pastrycooks' Staircase or the Riding Stables tract.

The long and colourful history of Schönbrunn Palace, together with its outbuildings and spacious park, makes it one of the most important cultural monuments in Austria. The building and its magnificent interiors, dating mainly from the time of Maria Theresa unite in their stylistic homogeneity both the ceremonial grandeur of an imperial palace and the domestic needs of the imperial family.

The history of Schönbrunn and the buildings that formerly stood on this site goes back to the Middle Ages. In the 14th century it is documented that there was a property named the Katterburg on this site, which consisted of a mill with a farmstead and outhouses. In the 16th century the Katterburg became a manorial estate.

The manor house with its working buildings came into Habsburg possession when Maximilian II acquired it in 1569. Maximilian's principal interest in the Katterburg lay in constructing a game enclosure for breeding fish and game, thus providing a suitable venue for the emperor's hunting parties.

The estate was badly damaged by plundering Hungarian troops in

View of the north façade of the »Lust und Thiergarten Schenbrunn« (pleasaunce and game park at Schönbrunn); copper engraving by Georg Matthaeus Vischer, 1672. The dowager empress Eleonora of Gonzaga used the hunting lodge to accommodate her hunting parties. On occasion theatre performances were given in the gardens.

1605, and the subsequent repairs proceeded only slowly.

In 1622 Emperor Ferdinand II placed the Katterburg at the disposal of his wife, Eleonora of Gonzaga, as a summer residence.

After Ferdinand's death in 1638, Eleonore settled permanently at the Katterburg, making it her dowager residence. In order to be able to lead an active social life there, she had a palatial tract added to the existing buildings in 1642/43. It was at this point that the estate acquired the name of »Schönbrunn« (beautiful spring), which allegedly goes back to the discovery of a »beautiful spring« by Emperor Matthias around 1615.

Schönbrunn and its park fell victim to the destruction that accompanied the Turkish siege of Vienna in 1683. In 1686 it was inherited by Emperor Leopold I, who decided to make it over to the heir to the throne, Joseph. He commissioned a hunting lodge from the architect Johann Bernhard Fischer von Erlach, who had received his training in Rome and become one of the most successful and sought-after architects at court and among the nobility. This hunting lodge was partially built on the still extant foundations of the tract added by Eleonora which had been destroyed by the Turks. By spring 1700 the central section of the lodge, known as the corps de logis and containing the living quarters, was completed and habitable. The building of the side wings was delayed on account of the War of the Spanish Succession and the resulting lack of funds. Work came to a complete standstill following Joseph's death in 1711.

As is typical for a Baroque palace, the whole ensemble is dominated by a central axis. On this axis in front of the central section was the ceremonial stairway which led directly up to the *piano nobile*. The lower part of these stairs was a carriageway, enabling coaches to drive up halfway.

The state rooms of the hunting lodge lay on the courtyard side, the private apartments of Joseph I on the garden side in the west wing of the palace, while the east wing was used for the accommodation of guests.

The reign of Maria Theresa represented an epoch of splendour for Schönbrunn Palace. Under her personal influence and the direction of the court architect Nikolaus Pacassi, the former hunting lodge of Joseph I was rebuilt and extended into a palatial residence. In the winter of 1742/43 work began on the huge project of rebuilding which was eventually to result in the palace that to a large extent looked as it does today.

The first phase of the rebuilding from 1743 to 1749 concentrated on

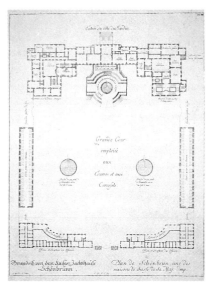

Ground plan of the hunting lodge at Schönbrunn by Johann Bernhard Fischer von Erlach.

Prospect of the hunting lodge at Schönbrunn by Johann Bernhard Fischer von Erlach. Fischer's hunting lodge is characterised by a compact central building with a corps de logis and side projections with a square courtyard situated immediately in front of it. This is bordered by side tracts for stabling and an entrance decorated with obelisks. Behind the palace the gardens extend to the wooded hill in the distance. A belvedere was planned for this hill as the crowning element of the park.

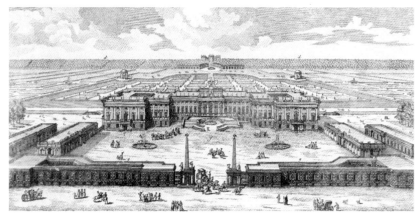

Engraving by G. Nikolai, 1749. The enlargement of the palace by the construction of extensive outbuildings became necessary during Maria Theresa's reign when she started to use Schönbrunn as her summer residence and additional space was needed for the accommodation and provisioning of the imperial household.

the east wing containing the audience chambers and residential apartments for the future imperial couple, which were completed in 1745. By 1748 the new mezzanine floor of the east wing, which housed the imperial children and their household, was also finished.

It was during this phase that Fischer von Erlach's monumental external stairway was demolished in order to create a spacious open passageway on the ground floor. At the same time, the Blue Staircase was erected in what had been the dining room in the west side wing in Fischer von Erlach's palace, as a ceremonial entrance to the *piano nobile*, but without destroying the original articulation of the walls of Erlach's dining room on what had been the first floor and thus also preserving the ceiling fresco painted by Sebastiano Ricci in 1702/3.

In the central section of the palace Pacassi created the Small and Great Galleries, for use on ceremonial occasions of various kinds, whether on a large scale or in more private circles. On private occasions, direct access to the Great Gallery was afforded by the sweeping flights of the Hofstiege (Court Staircase); on official occasions, in observance of court ceremonial, guests had to walk the long way round from the Blue Staircase to the audience chambers of the imperial couple.

To accommodate her rapidly increasing family, Maria Theresa was compelled to extend the palace once more. In this second phase of building, from 1753 to 1763, an intermediate floor was inserted into the west wing to create space for the increasing numbers of children and their households. Alterations to the façades on the courtyard and garden sides completed this phase.

It was during this period that the Small and Great Galleries were decorated with magnificent stuccowork and frescoes, creating two of the most important interiors of the Rococo age.

After the death of Emperor Francis I Stephen in 1765, which was a particularly grievous blow to Maria Theresa, there followed a further period of refurbishment. The widowed empress

Façade facing the Parade Court; Bernardo Bellotto, known as Canaletto, 1759 (Kunsthistorisches Museum, Vienna). The painting shows the bustling activity in the Parade Court occasioned by the residence of the court in summer. The carriage at the centre of the picture represents a current event: it is carrying a messenger bearing the news of the Austrian victory at Kunersdorf (August 12th 1759) to Maria Theresa.

The palace from the gardens; painting by Bernardo Bellotto, known as Canaletto, 1759 (Kunsthistorisches Museum, Vienna). Canaletto's love of detail is shown in the figures of the promenading ladies-in-waiting as well as in the court gardeners going about their work in the park. The painting is also the earliest surviving and accurate record of the garden façade of the palace.

The Great Gallery was used for large-scale celebrations and banquets. Franz Joseph preferred the adjoining Small Gallery for official banquets and dinners. In his old age he used to promenade in the Great Gallery in winter instead of the garden and had the room specially heated for this purpose. Electric lighting was installed in the palace in 1900, entailing the use of 1,104 lightbulbs in the Great Gallery alone.

had several rooms in the east wing of the palace fitted up with precious Chinese lacquer panels, paper wall-hangings and valuable wooden panelling, some of them as memorial rooms to her late husband.

Maria Theresa's last project was the laying out of the gardens in the 1770s, which she entrusted to the court architect, Ferdinand Hetzendorf von Hohenberg. It was he who was responsible for giving the park the form it still has today, with the Gloriette, the Neptune Fountain, the Roman Ruins and the obelisks.

Between 1817 and 1819, during the reign of Emperor Franz II (I), the façade of the palace was extensively altered after designs by the court architect Johann Aman, who removed the ornate Rococo decoration of Pacassi's façade. Today the exterior of the palace looks much as it did when these alterations were completed.

In 1830 Franz Joseph was born in the east wing of the palace, which contained the apartments used by his parents, Franz Karl and Sophie. He also spent the summer months of his childhood at Schönbrunn. During the course of his reign the palace became his favourite residence, where he spent a large part of his life, and it was here that he died, on November 21st 1916.

On his ascension to the throne in 1848, Franz Joseph moved into the chambers on the Parade Court side of the east wing. These formed a continous suite of rooms consisting of an audience chamber, a study and a bedroom. Official access to these apartments was via the Blue Staircase; the Gardezimmer and the Billiards Room served as *anticamere*, while the Walnut Room was used as the actual

The emperor's English water closet. Franz Joseph's aversion to technological progress led him to have the telephone installed in the toilet rather than in his study.

audience chamber. The precious wooden panelling and the console tables attached to the wall are from the time of Maria Theresa, while the furniture was made for Franz Joseph. The adjoining study and bedroom display the emperor's preference for a more modest and rather bourgeois style. The furniture in both these rooms was suppiled by the court cabinet-maker Heinrich Dübell.

The »English water closet« in the recess between the double doors was not installed until 1899.

Ahead of Franz Joseph's forthcoming marriage to Elisabeth, alterations were begun for the new empress in the winter of 1853 in the west wing facing the Hietzinger Kammergarten. The »Elisabeth Apartments« consisted of several rooms centred around the empress's salon. Here she received her personal guests, who arrived via the Blue Staircase, the Gardezimmer and the *anticamera* of the empress.

Towards the north, adjoining the salon, were the matrimonial bedchamber, the dressing-room and the study, forming the private chambers of the imperial couple, which were connected to Franz Joseph's apartments via the so-called Terrace Cabinet. A dividing wall was erected in the bedroom as early as the 1860s, as Elisabeth was constantly disturbed by the noise from the White Staircase, which was used by the servants.

Towards the south or garden side of the palace the Empress's salon adjoins the rooms used for family gatherings; the Antoinette Room was used as a dining room, the room known as the Children's Room was used as a family drawing-room. On the side facing the garden were the rooms known as the empress's »Kommandationszimmer«, which were used for official ceremonial purposes.

Elisabeth's life as the future Empress of Austria began at Schönbrunn. After her arrival in Vienna on April 22nd 1854, the emperor's young bride spent the first night at the palace. The next day she set out from

The empress's reception room; watercolour by Franz Heinrich, c. 1855/60. The salon was furnished and decorated in the neo-Rococo style which predominated at Schönbrunn, with white and gold panelling on the walls and matching furniture upholstered in red damask.

The marital bedroom; recent photograph. The heavy, dark rosewood furniture in this room and those adjoining it corresponded to contemporary fashion but probably not to the personal taste of the empress. The walls were hung with blue and white silk.

here for the official, ceremonial entry into the city.

Empress Elisabeth spent the first years of her married life partly at Laxenburg, but after 1860 she spent increasing periods at Schönbrunn. In 1862 a spiral staircase (today no longer in existence) was installed in her study, which afforded direct access to the rooms on the ground floor and gave the room the name by which it is known (i.e. the »Staircase Cabinet«). The rooms on the ground floor beneath the empress's apartments were refurbished for Elisabeth in 1863 as her exclusively private domain, with direct access to the gardens. As at Gödöllő in years to come, there was a large salon, and most probably an exercise room as well. A fireplace made of Carrara marble was installed, with the wall-hangings and upholstery in her favourite shade of lilac. At first there were only two rooms, but in 1864 a third room was added together with a terrace to the private garden of the imperial family.

Elisabeth's children also lived on the ground floor of the palace. Her elder daughter Gisela occupied rooms on the garden side, while in 1867 Rudolf was allocated the Crown Prince Apartments, which gave onto the Crown Prince Garden, on the Meidling side of the palace.

After Elisabeth had largely abandoned her official duties over the course of time through her frequent absences, the family rooms in the Elisabeth Apartments on the *piano nobile* were placed at the disposal of her youngest daughter, Marie Valerie. Following her marriage to Archduke

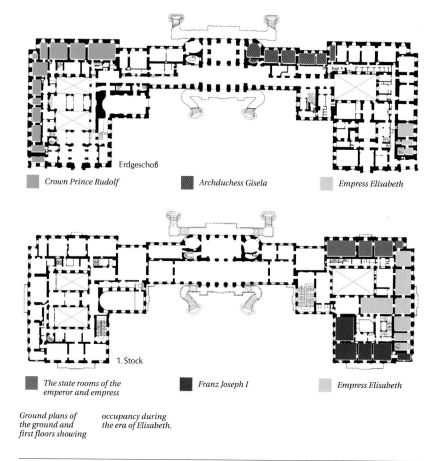

Erdgeschoß

Crown Prince Rudolf   Archduchess Gisela   Empress Elisabeth

1. Stock

The state rooms of the emperor and empress   Franz Joseph I   Empress Elisabeth

Ground plans of the ground and first floors showing occupancy during the era of Elisabeth.

Elisabeth's study (known as the »Staircase Cabinet«) with the spiral staircase and the posthumous portrait of the empress by Franz August von Kaulbach; photograph after 1898. The spiral staircase, which had been installed at Elisabeth's wish, was removed around 1920/25. The portrait eventually came into the collections of the Bundesmobiliendepot.

Franz Salvator in 1890, Valerie moved into the western Kavalier tract, which from then onwards has been known as the Valerie tract. The rooms she had previously occupied were incorporated into the Ceremonial Apartments.

Elisabeth resided at Schönbrunn during the 1860s and 1870s. The palace park and a circus ring in the Winter Riding School gave the empress ample opportunity of practising her favourite sport of riding.

Later, after she had given up riding for good, she would spend as much time as possible walking in the gardens with a companion, such as Christomanos, her Greek tutor.

After Elisabeth's death in 1898 her apartments were left unoccupied. The spiral staircase in her study was removed after the end of the monarchy, and the garden rooms on the ground floor adapted so that they could be let.

Schönbrunn Palace has belonged to the Republic of Austria since the end of the Habsburg monarchy. Since 1992 it has been administered by the Schloss Schönbrunn Kultur- und Betriebsges. m. b. H.

The palace is one of the most important destinations on the international tourist circuit. However, even during the monarchy it exercised a great attraction for the general public. The gardens were opened to the Viennese for recreation in 1779, during the reign of Maria Theresa, and the palace itself could also be viewed by arrangement with the palace governor when the empress was not in residence. During the latter part of Emperor Franz Joseph's reign there were even guided tours of the uninhabited rooms in the palace.

Franz Joseph and
Elisabeth on the
terrace of the
Gloriette with the
garden façade of
the palace in the
background; steel
engraving by Ignaz
Lechleitner, 1855.

Elisabeth on horse-
back in front of the
Neptune Fountain
accompanied by
one of her dogs. A
portrait of her dog,
Oskar, hung in
Elisabeth's garden
apartments at
Schönbrunn on the
ground floor. There
was also a marble
statue of a Scottish
greyhound which is
probably identical
to the one today in
the imperial villa
at Ischl that was
formerly in the
Hermes Villa.

Towards the end of the Second World
War, the palace and the Gloriette were
severely damaged by bombardments.
An ambitious rebuilding programme
ensured that the destruction was repaired in a very short space of time.

In 1997 the palace and park of
Schönbrunn were included in the
UNESCO register of World Heritage
Sites.

The Imperial Dairy Farm at Schönbrunn

Ingrid Haslinger

In what was formerly the pheasantry of Schönbrunn Palace stands a building, today occupied by the Federal Educational and Research Institute for Horticulture, which was originally a huntsman's dwelling. The grounds surrounding the building were given to the imperial-royal huntsmen for their own use.

Empress Elisabeth was always extremely concerned to preserve her slender figure, and milk and other dairy products featured prominently in her diet. The empress collected cows of various breeds from all over Europe in order to find out which milk best suited her digestion. To this end a dairy farm was set up at Schönbrunn.

The huntsman's house was converted into a dairy farm with a byre for the empress's cows in 1895. An extension was built housing the byre, the milk room, the scalding-pantry and fodder store, as well as accomodation for the keeper. Space for a manure heap and a slurry pit were also included in the plans de-signed by the architect V. Edler von Weyman.

After the alterations were completed, the farm started producing milk and other dairy products, the surplus of which was sold to the general public. The dairyman was responsible for caring for the health and cleanliness of the animals. The dairy supplied the imperial court with full-cream milk, butter, cream and eggs, which had their own special stamp to show their provenance. In the so-called »milk chamber« the milk was scalded and cooled, bottled or skimmed, and butter and cream produced. To cool the milk two blocks of ice were delivered daily from the ice-house at Schönbrunn. Butter and cream was supplied daily to the court according to its needs. If special deliveries were needed, the pastry-chef on duty that day would send a note listing his requirements, or simply ring the dairy up, as it had its own telephone. It was not only the imperial family who enjoyed the milk; Katharina Schratt and Ida von Ferenczy also received their share.

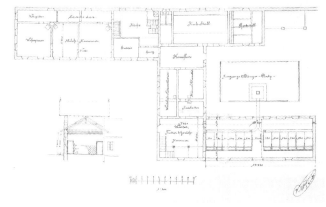

Far left: Exterior of the imperial dairy farm, recent photograph.

Ground plan of the imperial dairy farm (Haus-, Hof- und Staatsarchiv, Vienna).

Furniture from the empress's dining room (Museen des Mobiliendepots, Vienna).

Besides the dairy rooms, the byre and the living quarters for the dairyman, the building also contained rooms for the empress: an anteroom, a dining-room and a dressing-room. The dining-room is of particular interest, as the empress had it furnished and decorated like a Hungarian peasant's parlour. The softwood furniture was painted red with flower motifs. The dinner and tea services were of Hungarian manufacture and were also decorated with flowers. The table linen and curtains continued the Hungarian peasant theme with their red or blue stripes, finished with the monogramme *I.M.K.* (*Ihrer Majestät Kammermeierei*; Her Imperial Majesty's Dairy Farm), topped by an imperial crown. Photographs of Hungarian cows, statuettes and around 20 pictures of various cattle breeds, mostly painted by Julius Blaas, decorated the walls of the rooms. The dining-room, which in its original state probably had plain wooden panelling, has murals of country scenes, painted by the court scene painter, Anton Brioschi.

The dairy farm was a favourite haunt of the empress. Other members of the imperial family also enjoyed walks in this part of the palace park, which was closed to the general public. Until the death of the empress, the dairy was run by Ida von Ferenczy; thereafter it was taken over by the Imperial Family Fund. After 1916 it was assigned to the office of Empress Zita's *Obersthofmeisterin*. The furnishings remained untouched. Even after the collapse of the monarchy the dairy continued to produce and played an important part in maintaining fresh milk supplies in Vienna during the Second World War and the post-war period. It eventually closed down in 1960. During the course of restoration work the cow byre was converted into a classroom and rooms for work and recreation, whereby the original supporting cast iron pillars were preserved. The meadow where the cows used to graze was turned into horticultural land. An orchard and vegetable garden were also laid out in the grounds of the former imperial dairy farm.

The Imperial Villa at Bad Ischl
– imperial summer residence and hunting lodge in the
Salzkammergut

Monika Oberhammer

View of the Villa Eltz which Archduchess Sophie bought for her son in 1854. Conversion of the villa for the imperial couple started in 1855; painting by Thomas Ender, 1836.

The Seeauer family house, later the Austria Hotel, where Elisabeth and Franz Joseph celebrated their engagement.

»Joyful was the day for the inhabitants of Ischl, a day that will never be forgotten, for in a thousand years from now, Clio's golden letters will shine in the annals of Ischl and speak to posterity: on this day in Ischl, in the house of the Mayor, Wilhelm Seeauer, His Imperial-Royal Apostolic Majesty Franz Joseph I, Emperor of Austria, was betrothed to Her Royal Highness, the illustrious Duchess Elisabeth Eugenia, Princess of Bavaria; after this solemn act, in order to implore God's blessing, both of Their Majesties attended Holy Mass at 11 o'clock in the church of this parish.« Thus were the events of August 19th 1853 recorded in a chronicle written by one Joseph Ramsauer.

The Seeauers' house on the banks of the River Traun, Esplanade No. 10 (which later became the Austria Hotel and from 1985 has housed the local museum) had been let to the imperial family ever since they had started taking regular bathing cures in Bad Ischl from 1827. However, local commercial accommodation was unable to cope with the ensuing influx of prominent visitors from all parts of the monarchy and official guests from all over the world, so that private quarters had to be sought. The most suitable houses for this were the imposing saltwork owners' houses on the River Traun.

The mayor, Wilhelm Seeauer, also belonged to an ancient family of saltwork owners who had lived on the Traun since the 17th century. At the ball given on August 17th by the Seeauers to mark the emperor's 23rd birthday, Franz Joseph fell in love with his cousin Elisabeth, and the very next day, the actual date of his birthday, asked for her hand in marriage.

The following year Archduchess Sophie purchased a property for the imperial couple from a Viennese notary, Dr. Josef August Eltz, where Franz Joseph hoped to live henceforth »in complete privacy« with Elisabeth.

View of the imperial villa after conversion. The old Villa Eltz was incorporated into the central section where Elisabeth had her apartments. Two new side wings were added; the west wing (on the left) was occupied by Franz Joseph, while the children had rooms in the east wing (on the right); historical photograph.

The conversion and adaptation of the imperial summer villa was initially entrusted to Antonio Legrenzi, imperial-royal groom of the chamber »who has already distinguished himself in several achievements of an architectural nature«. Following the latter's death in 1858, the work was completed in 1865 by Franz Rauch, imperial-royal court gardens inspector, who was also active at Ofen and Laxenburg.

The grounds of the imperial summer residence extended from the peak of the thickly-wooded Jainzen mountain, north of Ischl, which was ideal chamois-hunting country, to its spurs, which terminate gently in meadows before falling sharply to the River Traun. The gardens of the villa were also laid out by Rauch, who had studied modern garden design in England and France. He was especially concerned to create smooth transitions from the house, via the flower-beds in front of it with their careful plantings of tropical and western European flora, such as heliotrope, geraniums, roses, palms and banana trees, to the indigenous forest on the Jainzen.

Access to the villa is via unobtrusive wrought-iron gates up a gently-sloping drive lined with lamp-posts decorated with the imperial crown which leads obliquely to the villa itself. The outhouses – stables, coach-houses, a dairy farm – are on the right,

concealed behind trees. The estate is today still in the possession of the Habsburg-Lothringen family.

The villa is a two-storeyed building, strictly symmetrical in both ground-plan and elevation, with its main façade facing the park and the mountain. The central section is formed by the original Eltz villa, a porticoed cube with a projecting centre. To this were added connecting wings and side sections in the same style as the central section. The exterior and interior decoration are far removed from the pomp and grandeur of the imperial style, and give no indication as to the rank of the villa's owner.

Hunting motifs decorate the three gables, while hunting trophies, together with paintings and statuettes of hunting scenes, predominate in the hall, on the staircase and in the corridors.

The empress's apartments are in the central section of the villa. The room she used as her breakfast salon faces north, looking out towards the park, while her Red Drawing Room faces south. The bedroom, bathroom and boudoir are on the east side, followed by the children's rooms, her study and dressing-room on the west side, adjoining the emperor's apartments. All the rooms today contain mementoes of Elisabeth: portraits not only of herself but also of her favourite daughter Valerie (who celebrated her wedding in Ischl), of her

The empress's Red Salon; recent photograph.

The emperor's study; recent photograph.

sister Mathilde, as well as of her horses and dogs. In the chapel there are various »relics«, such as her bridal handkerchief, the pillow on which she died, together with the emperor's funeral bouquet.

Winding paths lead away from the villa, with picturesque groups of trees revealing ever-changing vistas. View points and resting-places invite the visitor to linger awhile: a mirror pavilion, a »Turkish« kiosk and the »Cottage«, known as the »Marble Castle«. Built of blocks of pink marble in the »English Elizabethan style«, it is surrounded by a terrace with a cast-iron fence whose tendrilled patterns imi-

tate the natural forms of its setting. In the interior, known as the »Grand Salon«, wooden figures representing the protagonists of the Nibelung saga are ranged around the walls, culminating in the Habsburg dynastic arms, which are mounted above the entrance.

For Emperor Franz Joseph, Ischl was always »heaven on earth«, a place where every summer he fled from his »desk-bound paper existence with all its cares and troubles«, the place he longed for when Schönbrunn »which I cannot bear in any case« became »quite intolerable« on account of the summer heat, as Franz Joseph wrote to his mother (letters of September

View of the Cottage or »Marble Castle«, built in the historic-Romantic style with pink marble facing; photograph.

The Marble Castle; view from the Large Salon into the garden; photograph, 1977.

A family dinner at the imperial villa; drawing by Theo Zasche after a photograph by Angerer and Göschl, c. 1890.

6th 1853, August 30th 1856, September 28th 1868).

The fact that Ischl was also a very special place for Elisabeth is revealed in a poem that she dedicated to her daughter Valerie, and which she must have composed while walking on the Jainzen, »Mama's magic mountain«, as Valerie used to call it:

Oh spread thine arms
Maria, as we greet thee!
Lay them protectively on this house
In the vale at thy feet!
Oh bless this little place,
Though the storm rage,
In thy protection it stands fast,
Full of mercy, thou wilt keep watch
over it …

The empress stayed regularly at Ischl, sometimes having her horses sent to join her. She enjoyed hiking in the mountains, especially with Valerie; at times these hikes were so arduous that her ladies-in-waiting were almost unable to keep up with her.

On July 15th 1898 the empress left Ischl to take the waters at Bad Nauheim. Franz Joseph would never see his wife alive again.

On July 17th he wrote to her from Ischl: »I think with pain on the endlessly long time we will be apart; the sight of your rooms, emptied of all your things, makes me particularly sad …«

On September 15th women from Bad Ischl went to the nearby railway junction at Attnang in order to put a wreath on the funeral train that was bearing the body of Empress Elisabeth from Geneva to Vienna.

The Hermes Villa at Lainz
– imperial hunting lodge –
neither home nor refuge for Elisabeth

Peter Haiko

»Panoramic view of the Villa Waldruh«; watercolour, signed and dated »Hasenauer 18. 12. 1881« (Historical Museum of the City of Vienna).

»Front view of the Villa Waldruh«; never constructed; watercolour, signed and dated »Hasenauer 18. 12. 1881« (Historical Museum of the City of Vienna).

»In the immediate vicinity of the imperial capital, and yet in quiet seclusion at the heart of a glorious natural park lies a wondrous *buen-retiro*, the »Hermes« Villa, given as a gift to our Empress of cherished memory [...] by her imperial consort. [...] If one were to summarize the impression that the external appearance of this imperial villa makes as a whole, one would say that, apart from its unusual dimensions, it does not differ in any way from the image of the country house belonging to a wealthy private individual, and in this the artistic creator of the whole, the architect Baron Hasenauer, has faithfully fulfilled the intentions of his imperial patron. As soon as one enters the interior of the villa, however, it is proclaimed from all the walls and ceilings that one is in the residence of a ruler and his consort, to whom art has become an absolute desire of the heart with which, even in their private family home, in the quiet solitude of country life, it neither can nor will dispense.«

Thus the description of the villa in *Franz Joseph I. und seine Zeit* (Franz Joseph I and his Times), a cultural and historical review of the emperor's reign, which was intended as a celebratory publication on the occasion of the 50th jubilee of the emperor's reign and appeared in 1898, the year Empress Elisabeth was assassinated.

It is not surprising that the Hermes Villa came to symbolise in architectural form the illusion of intact royal family life, being intended to contribute generally to the glorification of the monarch and his consort and supposedly attesting to the love of nature, mutual affection, modesty, love of art and the sense of family shared by Franz Joseph and Elisabeth. However, this was overrating the architecture to the same degree as when, ten years earlier, in *Die österreichisch-ungarische Monarchie in Wort und Bild* (The Austro-Hungarian Monarchy in Word and Image, a work published on the initiative of Crown Prince Rudolf), the villa had been celebrated as »the crown of modern palatial architecture in Lower Austria«.

The intensification of interest in Elisabeth's personality assigned the Hermes Villa a key role in the understanding of the empress's psyche. The villa then came to be seen as the »*buen retiro*« mentioned in the passage quoted above, but for the empress alone. Feeling at home neither in the Hofburg nor the magnificent rooms of Schönbrunn Palace, she allegedly »withdrew to the palace built for her in the game park at Lainz, near Hietzing.« The architecture of the villa built for »this strange woman« becomes for this particular author (whose work was intended to be »a commemoration of the late empress and queen«) the »castle of Sleeping Beauty in the enchanted forest, surrounded by an impenetrable thicket of thorns«. Encompassed by a wall of several kilometres, in the middle of the park at Lainz, which extends for miles around and to which access was only permitted to court servants, the empress created her own palace which remained »a secret to the whole world« and in which »from the very beginning everything was disposed according to her wishes and instructions«. This was the legend which sprang up almost immediately after her death.

The first designs for the Hermes Villa in the park at Lainz date from December 1881. The architect was Carl von Hasenauer, who had been entrusted with the completion of the Hofburgtheater as well as the court museums, and commissioned to build the Neue Hofburg. In his capacity as imperial-royal court architect he also presented a first set of designs for a »hunting lodge for His Imperial and Royal Majesty«, at this stage vaguely referred to as the »Villa Waldruh«.

The contracts for supplies of building materials and other items contained among the documents relating to the building of the Hofburgtheater and the court museums would seem to indicate that the villa, at least for purposes of administration, was classed with the new buildings being added to the Hofburg complex along the Ringstrasse which were financed by the Vienna urban development fund. There are orders signed personally by Hasenauer in the name of the »supervision of building works of the imperial-royal court museums and the imperial-royal court theatre« for the »building of His Majesty's hunting lodge in the imperial-royal game reserve« up to September 1883, that is, when the building was completed. From orders for manhole covers, sink traps, door frames for the cellar or stones for the terrace underlay to »pieces of quality marzano stone for the carved decoration« were all channelled through the office that had in fact been set up to supervise the construction of the monumental buildings belonging to the Hofburg complex on the Vienna Ringstrasse, and which was responsible to the urban development fund. It was thus no coincidence that the working plans for the villa were preserved in the designs archive of the Burgtheater. The construction company as well as many other firms employed in the construction of the villa were the same firms used for the other court buildings.

It is possible that the debate which broke out at this point on whether the court buildings on the Ringstrasse – erroneously regarded as being the

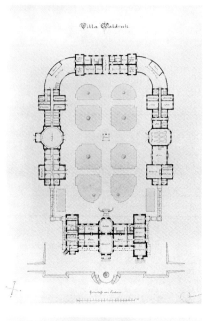

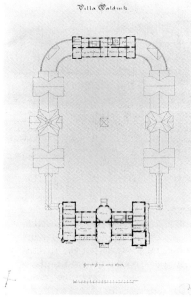

*Ground plan of
the ground floor,
signed and dated
»Hasenauer 26. 1.
1882« (Historical
Museum of the City
of Vienna).*

*Ground plan of
the first floor,
signed and dated
»Hasenauer 26. 1.
1882« (Historical
Museum of the City
of Vienna).*

private property of the emperor –
should in any case be financed by the
Vienna urban development fund, was
the reason why the hunting lodge
in the game park at Lainz, which belonged to the imperial court, was
transferred to the private possession
of Her Majesty Empress Elisabeth.
It was not until then that a proper
division was made between the property of the imperial court and the
private property of the Habsburgs in
respect of the villa. It thus passed from
the possession of the imperial court
and became the property of the royal
family. The purchaser was Empress
Elisabeth, vendor the *Oberjägermei-
steramt* (Office of the Grand Master of
the Hunt), an imperial court office
that until that juncture had certainly
had nothing to do with the duties relating to the new Hofburgtheater and
the imperial museums financed by
the Vienna urban development fund,
but whose common supervisory board
was at that time directing the construction of the hunting lodge in the
game park at Lainz.

Although the history of the construction of the Hermes Villa up to the
date of the contract of sale is unclear –
there exists neither a contract with the
architect nor any other documents –
all the receipts and accounts dating
from after the contract of sale are me-
ticulously recorded.

This incorporation of the villa
into the estate of Empress Elisabeth
has usually been regarded as an attempt by Emperor Franz Joseph to
bind his beloved wife to Vienna and
thus himself, and to create a refuge
for her which would accommodate
all her wishes and eccentricities. The
Hermes Villa was supposed to be
»Titania's faerie castle«, the embodi-
ment in architecture of Elisabeth's
desire to retreat from the world.

However, this assumption is not
borne out by the architectural design
of the villa or by the history of its construction. The plans submitted by Carl
Hasenauer at the end of 1881 for the
»Villa Waldruh« represent a uniquely
uninspired exercise in standard 19th-

The empress's salon; photograph by Lederer, c. 1898/99.

The empress's bedroom, known as the Makart Room. This is the only room at the villa which has been preserved largely in its original state. Since 1980 the other rooms of the Hermes Villa have been used for exhibitions put on by the Historical Museum of the City of Vienna; photograph by Lederer, c. 1898/99.

century villa architecture, with typical articulation into corner projections and a central projecting section on the two long sides, terminating in decorative lateral turrets. Although this orthodox façade was later relieved somewhat by giving it an assymetrical aspect in imitation of a »romantic« castle, Hasenauer had already determined the final internal division of space even at this early stage. This, too, has been copied straight out of a manual of court architecture as it were, being divided symmetrically into apartments for His Majesty on the left-hand side and for Her Majesty on the right-hand side, with identical

rooms of equal size for the studies and private quarters. Both apartments are divided by a central hall with an anteroom. The ground floor was originally intended to contain accommodation for guests but was converted into apartments for Archduchess Marie Valerie. The outhouses around the perimeter of the inner courtyard were reserved for stabling, kitchens and other offices.

The design of the villa reveals no trace of its patron's personality, representing rather the type of architecture that was the contemporary standard for a royal villa-cum-hunting lodge in a grand, rather urban and highly

The empress's dressing-room with a view of her exercise room; photograph by Lederer, c. 1898/99.

The emperor's study; photograph by Lederer, c. 1898/99.

The »Corfu Salon« on the ground floor which formerly belonged to Gisela's apartments. When the Achilleion was put up for sale in 1897 while Elisabeth was still alive, a part of the furniture from the Greek villa was transferred to the Hermes Villa; photograph by Lederer, c. 1898/99.

Archduchess Marie Valerie's study on the ground floor; photograph by Lederer, c. 1898/99.

The Hermes Villa at Lainz

impersonal style. The one deviation from the original design bears Elisabeth's mark: the separate exercise room. However, since at this period these were installed wherever Elisabeth resided it does not prove that the empress was in any way involved in the planning of the Hermes Villa as such. According to her definition, the villa was »His Majesty's hunting lodge«, that is, intended for Emperor Franz Joseph, and it was thus that it was officially referred to, even after it was transferred to Elisabeth's possession.

The decoration of Her Majesty's bedroom, which was designed by Hans Makart, has always been interpreted as having an especially significant bearing on Sisi's personality. The scenes from Shakespeare's *Midsummer Night's Dream* indubitably play on Elisabeth's personal affinity with the play; she sees herself as Titania in several of her poems, and had pictures of Titania hanging in all her residences. However, it is recorded that when she first viewed Makart's sumptuously decorated room she merely shook her head. Her daughter Valerie, who privately no doubt shared her mother's opinion, gave the following verdict on the Hermes Villa in 1890: »These marble reliefs, these voluptuous carpets, fireplaces of chased bronze, these countless putti and amoretti, the carving here, there and everywhere, this mannered Rococo style! I wish we were at home again.« Wherever home was, it was obviously not at Lainz.

That the Hermes Villa could not have been to Elisabeth's taste is illustrated by a comparison with the Achilleion on Corfu, which was built according to her true wishes. Here she really gave free rein to her longing and reverence for the ancient world, referred to by the court as her »Greek mania«. The villa at Lainz, on the other hand, was (and is) a psychogram of the emperor and his relationship with Elisabeth, if this largely mediocre architecture can be said to reflect anything at all of its patron's individuality.

It was the architect Carl Hasenauer and the artists Hans Makart and Viktor Tilgner who determined the appearance of the villa, and it was the emperor's predilection for an impersonal, rather bourgeois style of architecture which imprinted its stylistic stamp on the villa. By the time the imperial couple went to view the completed villa, Franz Joseph could not have failed to realise that his undemanding tastes were diametrically opposed to those of his wife. He could only note Elisabeth's rejection of the villa with resignation: »I will always be afraid of spoiling everything.« His wife and her enthusiasm for Greece were to remain a mystery to him: »I cannot imagine what you are doing all this time in Ithaca« he wrote in a letter to Elisabeth in 1887. He had wanted to make her happy with a gift of courtly neo-Baroque architecture and in this way to bind her more closely to Vienna.

There are few traces of Elisabeth's personality at the Hermes Villa. What there is is concentrated in the statue of Hermes by the Berlin sculptor Ernst Herter, erected in 1888, which she personally commissioned for the parterre of the garden and which gave the villa its name. The registry of the empress's private secretariat contains countless documents relating to this statue. It is significant that the villa, which was meant to be used for riding and shooting, was built just at the time when Elisabeth began to abandon these two sports of which she had formerly been so fond, and to replace them with lengthy hikes, which she indulged in no less excessively than in her previous occupations.

Elisabeth paid only obligatory visits to the Hermes Villa: »That's what is called »coming home«, she noted sadly in 1888 after she had arrived for one of these stays at the Hermes Villa, »but one is only at home where Nature is beautiful and people are gay«.

The Palace at Buda and the
Queen Elisabeth Memorial Museum
Beatrix Basics

The palace before work started on the rebuilding in 1875; photograph, c. 1860/70.

King Béla IV (1235–1270) founded a walled citadel on the plateau of the hill fortress of Buda following the Mongol incursions. A dwelling belonging to the royal court also stood on this site from the 13th century onwards. In 1347 King Louis the Great moved the royal court back to Buda from Visegrád. It was at this time that building started on the residential tower and the palace. During the course of the 14th century various buildings were added, including the two-storeyed chapel. Early in the reign of Sigismund of Luxemburg (1387–1437) new fortifications were built, while the south and east wings of the palace were completed at the beginning of the 15th century. In 1411 construction was begun on the »New Palace« which was altered and completed under Matthias Corvinus (1458–1490), who also extended the fortifications. Sources from this time repeatedly mention Italian architects in connection with the building work at Buda.

In 1526, following the defeat at the Battle of Mohács, the royal court fled from Buda and the palace was burnt down by the Turks. Between 1541 and 1686 the fortress at Buda was continuously in Turkish hands. During this time several parts of the palace were

destroyed, but the Turks also rebuilt other parts and constructed new buildings. After the fortress had been recaptured, Fortunato Prati was commissioned by King Charles III (Emperor Charles VI, 1711–1740) to draw up a plan of reconstruction for the castle. Prati designed a new palace using part of the old walls, but building did not properly begin until the reign of Maria Theresa (1740–1780). In 1749, the court architect Jean Nicholas Jadot, a Frenchman, produced new designs. From 1753 building was continued after plans by Nikolaus von Pacassi and completed after designs by Franz Anton Hillebrandt in 1760. At this time the palace was not used as a royal residence. Between 1762 and 1772 the building housed the Convent of the Ladies of Loretto, and from 1779 to 1784 the university at Nagyszombat occupied the palace at Buda. From 1790 it was used by the palatine in his capacity as regent.

In 1810 a conflagration broke out at the palace which was to be followed by a long period of alteration and reconstruction. During the siege of 1849, one of the most important military events of the revolution, the north wing and the central section were gutted by fire. In the 1850s the

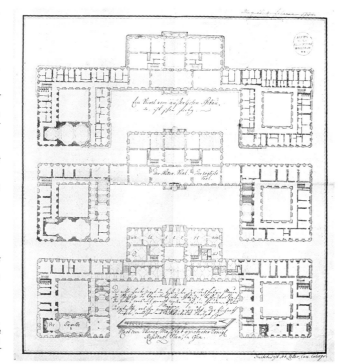

Ground plan of the palace during the conversion work carried out under Maria Theresa; drawing, signed and dated Seb. Zeller, 1758. After J. N. Jadot (from 1749), N. Pacassi took over supervision of the building work from 1753. Work was completed in 1770 after altered designs by F. A. Hillebrandt. This building today forms the southern wing of the section of the palace facing the Danube.

The fire that broke out in the night of May 13th 1849 and which destroyed the central section and the north wing; lithograph by A. F. Walzel, 1850/52 (National Museum of Hungary).

The palace garden »Bazaar«, inaugurated by Franz Joseph in 1881; photograph by Weinwurm, after 1880.

palace was partly rebuilt and enlarged after designs by the Viennese court architects Joseph Weiss and C. Weinwirth.

The Compromise of 1867 made the renovation and partial reconstruction of the palace imperative. This began in 1875 with the erection of outbuildings, to be followed by preparatory work for the building of the west wing after designs by Miklós Ybl, thus extending the palace deriving from Maria Theresa's reign. In 1881, Emperor Franz Joseph inaugurated the new »Burggarten Bazaar«, a spectacular series of terraces descending steeply to the Danube, which completely changed the appearance of that section of the riverbank. Ybl also had the idea for the complex of buildings which interrupts the fortifications on the Christinenstadt (Krisztinaváros) side. This complex is linked to the part of the Baroque palace facing the Danube by two wings which each have three axes.

After Ybl's death, Alajos Hauszmann assumed responsibility for the project

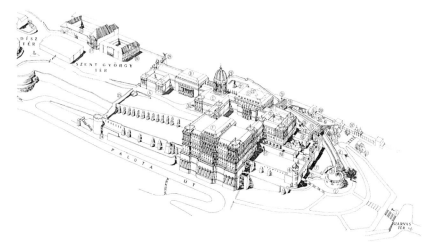

The king's breakfast room; photograph by Stillfried, 1886.

Bird's-eye view from the Christinenstadt; in the foreground is the complex of buildings designed by Ybl and executed by Hauszmann (housing the Széchényi Library) which was linked to the Baroque palace via two wings; drawing by Tamás Biczó, 1979.

The king's study in Buda Palace; photograph by Stillfried, 1886. Although Franz Joseph complained about the cold, particularly in his study, he hoped »to find a sanctuary to which

I can withdraw when the Viennese become really too vexing«, as he wrote to his wife on November 17th 1867. No historic photographs of Elisabeth's rooms exist.

The royal family in Hungarian costume with the palace in the background. On her lap Elisabeth holds Marie Valerie, who had

been born at Buda/ Ofen; lithograph, c. 1870.

Buda Palace after completion (1902) under the supervision of the architect Hauszmann. He had the dome constructed on top of the central section of the long complex of buildings.

in 1891, and work was completed under his supervision in 1902. Hauszmann continued the building of the Christinenstadt wing, laid out the large inner courtyard and enlarged the wing facing the Danube with a second projecting section towards the fortress quarter. However, this had the effect of making the central section of the complex recede. In order to compensate for this defect, Hauszmann emphasised the central section by adding an sweeping external flight of steps, an order of columns and a gable decorated with a statuary group. On the central axis he placed a false dome purely for decorative purposes. This solution, taken over by an Austrian architect from French architecture (a similar false dome is to be seen at the royal palace at Gödöllő), aimed primarily at external effect, as there is no corresponding interior domed space beneath its structure, its sole function being to emphasise the fact that this is the residence of a monarch. The dome originally had many decorative elements, just as the whole overly long complex of buildings was embellished with mansard roofs, dormer windows and projecting elements. Until the siege of Budapest during the Second World War, the imposingly ornate neo-Baroque exterior of the palace was one of the most important architectural creations in the Eclectic-Historicist style from the second half of the 19th century. The damage from the Second World War was repaired between 1948 and 1959, with archaeological excavations being carried out at the same time in the medieval part of the palace. Today the building appears considerably plainer than when it was originally built by Hauszmann.

The Queen Elisabeth Memorial Museum

On January 15th 1908, the Queen Elisabeth Memorial Museum was opened in the wing of Buda Palace that was designed by Hauszmann. The history of its foundation is to be found in a letter from Franz Joseph I to the Hungarian prime minister Sándor Wekerle dated November 14th 1907.

On December 1st 1898, the year of the empress's death, Gyula Wlassics, the Hungarian minister for Culture, Education and Religious Affairs, informed the director of the Hungarian National Museum in a letter that Gisela, Princess of Bavaria, and Archduchess Marie Valerie had made a gift to the Hungarian nation of a number of articles belonging to estate of their mother. The royal palace administration presented 45 objects to the director of the National Museum, chiefly messages of tribute addressed to the queen. In 1899 Ida von Ferenczy, Elisabeth's companion, presented the black gala robe that Elisabeth had worn on the occasion of the ceremony of homage held to mark the Hungarian millenium in 1896. Until 1907 these »relics« were held by the Collection of Antiquities of the Hungarian National Museum, where they were put on display. On March 11th of the same year, a committee composed of

ladies of the higher nobility travelled to Vienna and petitioned Franz Joseph for the furniture and memorial objects from the apartments of the empress to form the holdings, together with the objects until then preserved at the Hungarian National Museum, of a new memorial museum to be established at Buda Palace. The members of this committee, which was headed by the widowed Countess Leontin Andrássy, née Baroness Wenckheim, were Margravine Adele Pallavicini, née Countess Mailath, and Ilona Batthyány, née Countess Andrássy. The emperor entrusted Ida von Ferenczy, who was the person most intimately acquainted with the empress's possessions, with the selection of suitable objects as well as with the proposal for establishing the memorial museum. Franz Joseph also donated a memorial object, namely the small silver casket in which the deputation of the Hungarian provinces had presented their coronation gift in 1867. Marie Valerie donated the Hungarian books from Elisabeth's library as well as a number of commemorative objects, the latter together with Gisela. Ida von Ferenczy donated nearly one hundred objects, including portraits, statues, autographs, printed works and other commemorative objects. Elisabeth's lady-in-waiting, Countess Irma Sztáray, presented the clothes Elisabeth had been wearing when she was assassinated in Geneva. Countess Marie Festetics donated a plaster cast of a life-size statue of the queen together with various other objects to the museum. All these objects constituted the collection at the memorial museum, which consisted, according to Ida von Ferenczy's suggestion, of a room furnished entirely with the objects from the queen's former study, as well as a further exhibition room.

The museum was housed in rooms adjoining that where the Crown of St. Stephen was kept. Alajos Hauszmann himself designed the conversion of these rooms into a space suitable for a museum. The queen's former study was furnished with its original furni-

Elisabeth's study in the former Queen Elisabeth Memorial Museum; photograph, 1907.

The display room in the former Queen Elisabeth Memorial Museum; photograph, 1907.

The queen's writing-desk in the former Queen Elisabeth Memorial Museum; photograph, 1907.

ture under the personal supervision of Ida von Ferenczy, and the exhibition in the other room was completed with the objects from the National Museum. The inventory was drawn up by the members of the ladies' committee together with the architect and the director of the National Museum. All the objects as well as the Memorial Museum itself were placed under the aegis of the Hungarian National Museum, and a single-volume »descriptive catalogue« illustrated with photographs was also published.

As is often the case with memorial museums, the articles exhibited were very varied in both nature and quality. On the occasion of the king and queen's state visit to Hungary in 1857, a number of Hungarian artists had presented Her Royal Majesty with their paintings. Most of these paintings are genre pictures by well-known artists such as Károly Lotz, Mihály Szemlér, Bálint Kiss, Miklós Barabás, Mór Than or József Molnár. The correspondence between Elisabeth and Baron József Eötvös touchingly documents the queen's studies of the Hungarian language. She had asked Eötvös to correct her mistakes and in this way to improve her grasp of Hungarian grammar. The queen's prayer book was displayed open at the prayer *For the Well-Being of the Country*, and beside it was a portrait of the Hungarian statesman Ferenc Deák. There were also transcriptions of Hungarian works of literature in Elisabeth's hand, and it was no coincidence that the first one was Mihály Vörösmarty's patriotic poem entitled *Proclamation*. The large number of commemorative and portrait medallions included in the exhibition had been struck on the occasion of family events and state visits. Besides photographs, addresses to the queen and clothing, the documents relating to the death of the queen were also displayed, as well as numerous statues and articles of daily use, presented as if they were holy relics. In one corner of the reconstructed study the writing-desk was arranged as it was when Elisabeth had used it.

On the walls hung portraits of her children and members of her family. The authentic arrangement of the furniture and other items evoked the impression that the queen was still present and using them.

The memorial museum was completed by a smaller room containing literary reminiscences of the queen and her paintings collection; this room was accessible »mainly for persons engaged in research«, as the catalogue remarked.

The Queen Elisabeth Memorial Museum no longer exists today. Together with the rest of the palace, the rooms that it was housed in were almost completely destroyed by bombs during the Second World War. However, most of its exhibits are today in the collections of the Hungarian National Museum (divided between the Historical Paintings Gallery, the 20th Century Collection, the Textile Collection and the Collection of Medallions) and can frequently be seen in temporary exhibitions. Apart from the superb works of art which are on permanent loan to Gödöllő Palace, a number of items can be seen in the recently-opened permanent exhibition on the history of Hungary at the National Museum.

Gödöllő Palace
– the coronation gift of the Hungarian nation
Ferenc Dávid

In Hungary, the words »Queen Elisabeth« and »Gödöllő« are inextricably associated with one another and when used together evoke the »golden« age of the monarchy.

The palace, its park and the surrounding woodlands came into the possession of the Hungarian crown in 1867 and the use of them was given to the king and his consort as a coronation gift. The intention behind this gesture was to place a summer residence and hunting lodge at the royal couple's disposal in addition to the official royal residence of the palace at Buda and thus facilitate regular periods of residence in Hungary. This was one of the statutary conventions established by the Compromise with Austria, with which the demand of the Hungarian estates for a »truly Hungarian« king, a demand which had been reiterated at frequent intervals over the centuries at the meetings of the Diet.

It was at this time that Elisabeth began to plan changes in her life. She felt that her children had been taken from her and she had not been allowed to experience true motherhood. She also thought that she would be able to draw her husband closer to her again. As the setting for this imagined idyll she chose Gödöllő, a palace that was far from Vienna and unsuited to the official pomp she so hated, where she could limit the numbers of the royal household and personally choose the people who belonged to it, as well as determining the daily routine of the imperial-royal family.

And so she set about arranging this. The documents in the Imperial Archives frequently record changes made at Gödöllő to accommodate the queen's wishes. The diaries of her lady-in-waiting Marie Festetics record how Elisabeth formed her personal circle and spent her time with the members of this circle and her children, in particular with her »royal Hungarian daughter« Marie Valerie, who was born at Buda in 1868. Vinzenz

Far left: main façade of the palace, recent photograph.

The royal family in the park at Gödöllő; lithograph by Vinzenz Katzler, 1871.

Axonometric drawing of the palace at Gödöllő as it is today; drawing by R. Kralovánszky.

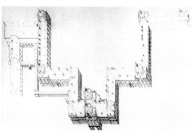

Katzler's painting of the royal family in the park at Gödöllő depicted an idyll that corresponded to Elisabeth's ideal. Behind the figures seated on garden furniture is the Baroque palace with its rounded domes. For Hungarians this painting recalled the monarch who for them had been the most memorable of the Habsburg rulers: Queen Maria Theresa.

Gödöllő was built by Anton Grassalkovich (1694–1771), a confidant of Maria Theresa and one of the organisers of the declaration of support known as »vitam et sanguinem«, proclaimed by the Hungarian Diet in Pressburg in 1741, which played a crucial part in strengthening the queen's position in the struggle to preserve her succession to the Austrian throne. Grassalkovich had risen from the ranks of the impoverished minor nobility to become a count and the owner of huge estates, from earning his living as an attorney to becoming Chancellor of the Hungarian Exchequer. His estates were grouped around an insignificant village called Gödöllő,

where he built a small, one-storeyed country house as a retreat from his town house in Pest in the 1730s. In 1743, the year he was made a count, he added a second storey and between 1746 and 1749 he had the palace extended so that it eventually had five wings. A visit of several days paid by Maria Theresa to Gödöllő in August 1751 ensured that the name of the palace would go down in Hungarian history.

Grassalkovich continued to extend the building right up to the end of his life, so that by 1771 Gödöllő was one of the largest palaces in Hungary. Seven wings were grouped in a double U-shape enclosing an ornamental garden in the French style. Close by there was a second courtyard for the stables and riding school, together with a third courtyard for the coach-houses and the palace brewery, as well as a fourth which was part of the estate farm.

The palace was built on a gently sloping artificial rise, the front of which was formed by fortress-like retaining walls. It thus stood above the village, its two-storeyed façade articulated by 31 windows and its corners still flanked at that date by slender towers. The restrained yet graceful building was designed by the Salzburg architect Andreas Mayerhoffer (1690–1771), while the projecting central section with its two domes was built by Nikolaus Pacassi (1716–1790), who was also responsible for the monumental

main staircase of the palace and the Great Hall (c. 1758). With its walls, cased in artificial white marble, and its gilded decoration beloved of Viennese and French taste, the Great Hall represents a typical example of the courtly art of Maria Theresa's age.

Anton Grassalkovich's son, also called Anton, was raised to the rank of prince by Emperor Joseph II and is known to the Viennese for the summer palace he had built in the Augarten park. He had the corner towers at Gödöllő replaced with projections and a theatre built in one of the side wings. His son, Anton III, who was the last male Grassalkovich, had the part of the village in front of the palace demolished and the lower park laid out, thus connecting the palace with the game reserve and beyond that with the woodland, so that it was completely surrounded by nature.

In 1867 work began on refurbishment and alterations for Franz Joseph and Elisabeth under the supervision of the court architect Ferdinand Kirschner. This mainly affected the side wings, where offices and living quarters were built for the imperial staff who accompanied the court on its travels. A separate coach house was built for the increased number of carriages, while the farmstead was replaced by kitchens, including a special one only for pastry and cake-making. The *Hofmeisteramt*, the office

Above: the palace c. 1867; historic photograph. In a letter of August 9th 1866, i.e., one year before the coronation, Franz Joseph urged Elisabeth to abandon her wish of buying the palace for reasons of economy.

Centre: design by Nikolaus Pacassi for the decoration of the Large Salon; pen-and-ink drawing, c. 1756 (Museum of Hungarian Architecture, Budapest).

Below: The Great Hall in the central section of the palace, recent photograph.

Elisabeth's salon; photograph, before/c. 1901.

Franz Joseph's study; photograph before/c. 1896. On November 27th 1867 the king wrote to his wife: »[...] my rooms are really so charming, so simple and yet élégant. [...] Only pictures are missing, which I will see to.«

that administered the imperial household, was also housed here.

The king and queen had their apartments on the first floor of the main building: Franz Joseph was given a small number of large rooms, while Elisabeth had several smaller rooms. The 18th-century reception rooms remained largely untouched, and where alterations proved necessary these were carried out in a neo-Rococo style which matched the original decoration. The expression of contemporary taste was mostly confined to items such as wall-hangings and curtains. The king's rooms and furniture were fitted out in carmine red, while those belonging to Elisabeth were done in her favourite shade of lilac. The furniture was simple to the point of being almost in bourgeois taste, and together with the pictures on the walls emphasised the intimate, family atmosphere of the palace. These pictures reflected the pleasurable occupations pursued by the king and queen when they were in residence here: Franz Joseph's rooms were hung with hunting scenes and in Elisabeth's rooms were pictures of equestrian scenes and places that she enjoyed visiting on excursions.

On the ground floor of the palace a second suite of three salons opening onto the garden were refurbished for Elisabeth. Guests personally invited by the queen could enter them via stairs leading down from Elisabeth's salon on the first floor, while the queen entered them by means of a spiral staircase in her dressing room. Here in

*Above left: a recon-
struction of the
queen's rooms.*

*Above right: a re-
construction of the
king's rooms.*

*The queen depart-
ing for a ride from
the paddock at
Gödöllő; water-
colour formerly
owned by Elisabeth
(Historical Museum
of the City of
Vienna).*

these rooms furnished with circular
sofas and decorated with extravagant
flower-arrangments she received her
intimate friends, her own personal
»Hungarian court«.

From the garden apartments a
covered wooden walkway led to the
stables and riding school, which was
renovated during the 1870s. This part
of the palace was where the queen
spent her most pleasurable hours:
in the riding school she trained her
circus horses Flick and Flock and
perfected her riding skills. In the
stables were the beloved horses she
rode on her long excursions and her
superb hunters. Elisabeth continued
to come to Gödöllő for the riding
even after her illusions of rebuilding
her family life had died. In the 1880s
and 1890s she paid only brief visits to
Gödöllő. After her death her apartments were inherited by her daughter

Marie Valerie. Franz Joseph last visited
Gödöllő in 1910.

Between the two world wars the
palace was the summer residence of
the regent of Hungary, Miklós Horthy.
When in residence he was accompanied by the staff of the regent's office
and a mounted guard.

After 1945 the main building became a Soviet military hospital and
later a barracks for Hungarian troops,
and was eventually turned into an old
people's home. The other buildings
remained in the possession of the
Soviet army until 1991. Small-scale
restoration work on the palace began
in 1981, but it was not until the foundation of the Royal Palace of Gödöllő
Society in 1993 that the palace was
ultimately saved for posterity. The
society has had the main building
restored as a museum and is now
planning to convert the other build-

The circus ring; photograph, before/c. 1896.

The stables; photograph, before/c. 1896.

ings for tourism with financial support from foreign institutions.

The palace museum opened in the summer of 1996. The façade and all the most important interiors are now as they would have looked during the 18th century. With the help of contemporary accounts and photographs the apartments of Franz Joseph and Elisabeth have been restored to look as they did when they were used by the royal couple and furnished accordingly. The permanent exhibition is intended to give an impression of the royal family and life at court.

The Achilleion on Corfu
– Empress Elisabeth's Greek villa
Ingrid Haslinger

Exterior of the villa with the main façade seen at an oblique angle. The architect of the villa, which was completed in 1892, was the Neapolitan Raffaele Carito.

Alexander von Warsberg, Austrian consul on Corfu; photograph. Warsberg, who was introduced to the empress in 1885 by Baron Nopcsa, thought her »ugly, old, thin as a rake [and] badly-dressed«, and felt she was »not foolish [...]

but mad«. Over the years a deep friendship subsequently developed between the empress and Warsberg.

»One is literally enfolded in the shade of the olive trees [...]. Here no fearful feeling of loneliness that often moves us in our native forest holds sway; it is the silence, the seclusion of a familiar room. One knows oneself to be alone, but one does not feel thus [...]. Up there on the brow of the hill, outside the village, I stopped by the Villa Braila. The garden and house are simple, almost poverty-stricken [...]. But what man has omitted, heaven has granted, and though the house and its garden are a wilderness, I would rather spend my life there than in all the palaces of Vienna and Paris, never leave again, only gaze, observe and enjoy, breathe in the air and feast my eyes.« Thus did Baron Alexander von Warsberg, an expert on Greece, describe the Villa Braila on Corfu.

A love of Greece was a Wittelsbach family tradition: Empress Elisabeth's father, Duke Max of Bavaria, had travelled extensively in Greece and had a fine appreciation of its culture, while her cousin Otto had even been King of Greece between 1832 and 1862. Empress Elisabeth went about her studies in Greek literature with characteristic vigour: she learned both Ancient and Modern Greek and was a devotee of Homer's epics. In order to perfect her knowledge of the language, she engaged Greek scholars to read works of Greek literature aloud to her, including one named Constantin Christomanos, who left a description of the Achilleion in his diaries.

Empress Elisabeth's first visit to Corfu in 1861 had been prescribed by her physician for suspected consumption. On her next visit in 1888, Elisabeth stayed at the Villa Braila and was delighted with its situation. In the same year she announced to Emperor Franz Joseph that she regarded Greece as her future home: »Corfu is an ideal place to stay, the climate, walks in the unending shade of the olive trees, good roads and the glorious sea air […].« It was also in 1888 that Baron von Warsberg began to draw up plans for a villa for the empress.

However, it was not until a year later that Emperor Franz Joseph was able to fulfil his wife's wishes and buy the old, rather dilapidated Villa Braila near Gastoúri. By purchasing the neighbouring properties the grounds were extended to approximately 200,000 square metres. From 1890 Emperor Franz Joseph defrayed those costs of construction not already covered by the empress's private income from his private purse.

With Elisabeth's approval the plan was conceived of building the new palace in the Pompeian style. The building was executed by Raffaele Carito, a Neapolitan architect. It is certain that Empress Elisabeth had a major influence on the design of

Right: the Villa Braila which previously stood on the site of the Achilleion. The empress stayed here in 1888; sketch, probably from 1889 (Academy of Fine Arts, Vienna, Kupferstichkabinett).

Below: design by Theophil Hansen for the empress's villa on Corfu, signed and dated

»Th. v. Hansen/ Vienna, May 1889« (Academy of Fine Arts, Vienna, Kupferstichkabinett). Designs submitted by Hansen, one of the Ringstrasse architects, when a new architect was being sought following Alexander Warsberg's death. It is not known why Hansen was not given the commission.

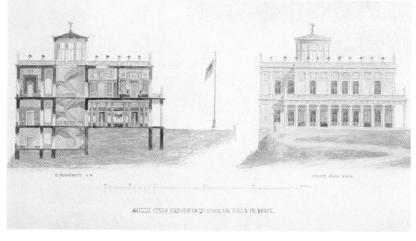

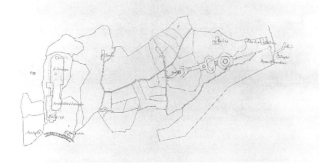

Map showing the villa and its outbuildings together with the landing stage (Haus-, Hof- und Staatsarchiv, Vienna).

Cross-section of the villa; newspaper illustration from »Über Land und Meer«.

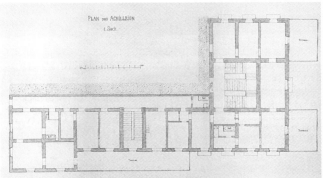

Ground plan of the top (i.e. second) floor with the rooms occupied by the empress (Haus-, Hof- und Staatsarchiv, Vienna).

the villa and its interiors as well as of the garden. After Alexander von Warburg's death in 1889, his brother, Baron Gustav von Warsberg, assumed the task of supervising the construction of the villa and the laying out of the gardens.

In 1890 Gustav von Warsberg relinquished his advisory duties, and his place was taken by Baron August von Bucovich. The laying out of the gardens was taken over by the Vienna court gardens director Anton Umlauft. He had large rosebeds constructed in deference to the empress's love of the flower.

The empress's palace was built on the slope of a high hill facing north

over the Bay of Benitses. Apart from the difficulties posed by the site, the architect also had to take the empress's romantic wishes for the palace into consideration: »I would like a palace with pillared halls and hanging gardens, sheltered from unwanted eyes – fabulous, proud, holy.«

At the front, where the main entrance is, the building has three storeys, diminishing to one storey at the back, which faces the garden. On the top floor was the exit to the peristyle, behind which stretched a large terraced garden with large trees. On the ground floor were the kitchens and a service lift. To the right beside

The Dolphin Fountain in the Garden of the Muses, photograph. Elisabeth chose the dolphin as the emblem of the Achilleion and had it marked on household items, such as the tableware.

the vestibule was the chapel. The first floor gave onto the terrace at the front of the villa. On the top floor were the empress's apartments, which gave directly onto the peristyle and faced south. The two wings of the peristyle enclosed the Garden of the Muses with the dolphin fountain. The statues of the nine Muses had been purchased by the empress in Rome from Prince Borghese. Two statues of wrestlers flanked the descent from the upper to the middle terrace. A statue of the dying Achilles by the Berlin sculptor Ernst Herter originally stood on the third garden terrace. The murals in the peristyle and in the villa itself were painted by the Neapolitan artists Paliotti, Postiglione and Scami after Pompeian models.

The whole property was surrounded by a high white wall. The empress had a landing stage of white marble constructed so that she could reach the villa in a small boat from her yacht, the *Miramar*. The mole of the landing stage was decorated with a stone dolphin. On a terrace of the slope leading up to the villa was the Heine Temple. An engine shed near the mole housed a generator for the electric illumination of the villa and

its garden. There was even an olive oil mill in the park, as there were many ancient olive trees on the estate, together with two glasshouses for plants.

Empress Elisabeth purchased a large part of the interior furnishings and decorations of the palace in Italy. Records show that a master cabinetmaker by the name of A. Capelli from Naples worked at the Achilleion, together with a Viennese cabinetmaker named F. Müller. The furniture was copied from Greek and Roman models. Each floor in the villa was equipped with bathrooms which had piped hot water, still an unusual feature for those times.

The Viennese artist Franz Matsch supplied two paintings for the Achilleion: *Achilles Triumphant*, which hung in the stairwell, and a Madonna painting entitled *Stella del mare* for the chapel of the villa.

In 1894 the sculptor Antonio Chiattone from Lugano was commissioned by the empress to create a monument for Crown Prince Rudolf in the garden of the Achilleion. Erected in April 1894, the main body of the sculpture was in the form of a cube with a socle supporting a broken chamfered column. On the front of the cube was a medallion with a portrait of the crown prince in half relief, above which a female genius spread its arms protectively. This monument was later erected at Mayerling and afterwards in the garden of the Rudolfstiftung in Vienna. The monument was severely damaged in the Second World War and only the medallion has survived.

After the villa had been completed in 1891, Baron Nopcsa, Empress Elisabeth's *Obersthofmeister*, wrote to Ida von Ferenczy: »The beauty of the place lies in the fact that it successfully combines the Pompeian style with modern comfort, without gold or the usual pomp; everything is simple, but very rich to the true connoisseur, since there is much art in it; expensive and rare stuffs upholster the furniture; the furniture of Their Majesties beautifully executed after Ancient Roman models [...] a property which will attract strangers hence to view this curiosity; I am only made sad by the thought of what future it will have, and for whom?«

One of the two hothouses in the garden of the villa; photograph, c./after 1890.

Nopcsa had a presentiment of what would happen: hardly was the Achilleion finished, when Empress Elisabeth lost all interest in it. She felt the villa to be a shackle which restricted her freedom of movement: »Our dreams are always more lovely if we do not realise them. When I was first on Corfu, I often visited the Villa Braila; it was glorious because it was quite abandoned in the midst of its huge trees. That drew me to it so strongly that I made the Achilleion out of it. Now I have to say that I regret having done so [...]. Wherever I were, if someone told me I had to stay there forever, then even paradise would become a hell for me.«

The empress's loss of interest was a source of great worry to Franz Joseph, as the building of the villa had been extremely costly. However, despite the emperor's admonitions, the villa was abandoned as a residence and put up for sale. In 1897 an estate agent was entrusted with the commission of selling the Achilleion. A large part of the furniture was shipped to Vienna, and two »Corfu« rooms were fitted up in the Hermes Villa.

After the empress's death in 1898, her elder daughter, Princess Gisela of Bavaria, inherited the villa, while Emperor Franz Joseph had the right of use to it for the rest of his life. However, the sale of the villa was delayed while the empress's estate was wound up and also because of the emperor's right of use to the villa. During the following years the upkeep of the villa was financed from imperial family funds.

Around 1905 offers were again made for the property. Many prominent persons all over Europe (among others the Rothschild family and the King of Greece), syndicates and businessmen made efforts to buy the Achilleion. All the interested parties tried to secure a reduction in the asking price.

In 1906 Emperor Wilhelm II of Germany let it be known that he was interested in the Achilleion. Princess

View of the peristyle terrace, known as the Garden of the Muses; to the left is the peristyle with the statues of the Muses. Most of these statues, which the empress believed to be originals from the classical age, were in fact 19th-century copies; photograph from the »Corfu Album«, c./after 1890.

The two wrestlers on the steps leading from the first to the second garden terrace are mirror-image replicas of a Greek original in the

Museo Nazionale in Naples; photograph, before/c. 1896.

The sculpture of the dying Achilles had stood in front of the Hermes Villa before it was shipped to Corfu. The motif of Achilles triumphant

was taken up by Franz von Matsch in his monumental painting for the stairwell of the villa; photograph, before/c. 1896.

Gisela and Emperor Franz Joseph were both delighted at this. The princess wrote to Wilhelm (who was her cousin) in 1907: »The Achilleion was put up for sale during my mother's lifetime; the fact that neither myself nor any members of my family proposed to use it was the reason that the reserve price was fixed at one million gold francs […]. Be assured that I would greet the knowledge of the Achilleion being in your hands with real joy – after all, I know how you adored my dear mother of whom you spoke to me with so much admiration […]«

On April 20th 1907 Franz Joseph relinquished his right of use to the Achilleion, and on May 26th of the same year Emperor Wilhelm assumed possession. A number of busts, bronzes and statues were sent back from the Hermes Villa to decorate the Achilleion. The costs of the refurbishment of the villa, which lasted until June, were defrayed from the private fortune of the Austrian emperor.

Emperor Wilhelm II did not have any extensive alterations made either to the house or the garden. However, between 1910 and 1914 it was slightly enlarged and furnished with simple cane furniture. At the foot of the villa he had a guest-house built. The sculpture of the dying Achilles was moved to the middle terrace and was replaced with *Achilles Triumphant* by the Berlin sculptor Johann Goetz. Wilhelm had the statue of the Heine in the small temple which Elisabeth had dedicated to her favourite poet removed and replaced with a statue of the empress herself. The statue of Heine came in a roundabout way to Hamburg and was eventually erected in the Jardin de Mourillon in Toulon in 1956.

In November 1918 Emperor Wilhelm II fled to Holland and there signed his abdication. The Achilleion became the property of the Greek nation after previously having served as an isolation hospital for influenza cases from the Macedonian army. During the military dictatorship of General Pangalos the interior furnishings disappeared, and the 1928 edition of Baedeker describes the Achilleion as being empty. In 1941 the villa be-

came a Greek military hospital and was subsequently occupied by Italian and German troops. After the Second World War the Achilleion served as accommodation for professors from the University of Technical Sciences in Corfu, and in 1962 the building was acquired by the Greek Casino Company. The Achilleion was restored, renovated and turned into a casino. A number of rooms on the ground floor were retained as a museum, which consists of the chapel and the memorial rooms for Empress Elisabeth and Emperor Wilhelm.

The museum is still open to the public. The casino, however, closed in 1993, and the villa today houses the offices of the Greek National Tourist Association.

Far left: the figure of the poet Heinrich Heine which previously stood in the small circular temple was replaced with a copy of the statue of Elisabeth by Edmund Hellmer by Emperor Wilhelm II, the later owner of the Achilleion.

Left: the memorial monument for Crown Prince Rudolf designed by Chiattone which (according to the

artist) was unveiled on April 22nd 1894, is one of very few monuments to be erected to the crown prince after his death (January 30th 1889). Today only the relief is still extant.

Above: the dining-room; photograph, before/c. 1896.

Below: the staircase of the villa; photograph, before/c. 1896.

Destinations

Feldafing, the Strauch Hotel, later the Empress Elisabeth Hotel; coloured newspaper wood engraving.

Combermere Abbey, Cheshire, 1881; newspaper wood engraving.

Elisabeth, King Ludwig II and the Tsar and Tsarina of Russia in front of the hydro at Kissingen, 1864; watercolour.

Trauttmansdorff Castle from the north; watercolour formerly owned by the empress.

*Miramar Castle;
painting by
Jankowsky/Wieser,
1868.*

*Archduke Johann's
villa in Gastein,
1851; lithograph.*

*The Rudolf Villa in
Reichenau on the
Rax; zincotype.*

*The Beau Rivage
Hotel in Geneva;
commemorative
postcard issued on
the occasion of the
empress's death.*

Madeira
– Elisabeth's first health cure
Elisabeth Hassmann

The Quinta Vigia, also known as the Quinta Angustia or Quinta Davies, at that time still situated outside Funchal, where Elisabeth stayed from the end of November 1860 to the end of April 1861. The villa was demolished to make way for a new casino in 1973.

Elisabeth in Funchal; heliotype by A. Dauthage; the face has been taken from a photograph by Ludwig Angerer. Elisabeth still wore crinolines at that period.

The year 1860 represented a caesura in the life of Elisabeth and in her relationship with Franz Joseph. In 1860 Elisabeth began to travel, an activity that she was to take to extremes after 1889 following the death of Crown Prince Rudolf. As early as 1859, when her husband was absent at the front in Italy, Elisabeth had begun to suffer from loneliness, which manifested itself in restlessness, insomnia, loss of appetite and an excessive need for exercise. In his letters Franz Joseph admonished his wife to rest but at the same time to make public appearances, above all to visit wounded soldiers in hospital.

Several factors contributed to Elisabeth's »flight« to Madeira at the end of 1860. Above all, she suffered from the domineering behaviour of her mother-in-law, Archduchess Sophie, who had seized charge of the upbringing of Elisabeth's children Gisela and Rudolf. Elisabeth had given birth to three children within four years, the eldest of whom, Sophie, had died at the age of two in 1857. The pain of this tragedy, as yet barely overcome, was compounded by the humiliation of her husband's adultery. The result of all this was a range of psychosomatic symptoms, including an alarmingly

View of the villa from the time Elisabeth stayed there; newspaper illustration.

severe cough. The pulmonologist Dr. Skoda recommended a warmer climate.

The empress's decision to travel to Madeira may have been prompted by Archduke Maximilian, who had travelled on the island and been very taken with it. On November 29th 1860 Elisabeth arrived at Madeira on the yacht *Victoria and Albert*, lent by Queen Victoria. On the island Elisabeth rented a country estate for a large sum of money. This estate was known variously as the Quinta Angustia, Quinta Davies or the Quinta Vigia. Surrounded by a park and with a view of the sea, it had one storey and at that time lay slightly outside the town of Funchal. It was used as a casino from 1956 to 1973, when it was demolished to make way for a larger casino on the same site. However, the park with its old trees was preserved and is now part of the Parque de Santa Catharina. The villa known today as the Quinta Vigia was originally called Quinta Lambert and is not the villa where either Elisabeth or Archduke Maximilian stayed.

Elisabeth led a very quiet life on Madeira, sometimes shutting herself up in her room for hours at a time. At other times she conversed with her ladies-in-waiting, played cards, learned to play the *macheta*, a small guitar typical of Madeira, or occupied herself with the domestic animals kept on the estate. »I have ordered a great big dog from England to have more companionship and which shall accompany me everywhere«, Elisabeth wrote to Count Grünne (quoted from Hamann). »If I had known what it was like here, I would have rather have chosen another place for such a long time«.

On April 28th 1861 she left Madeira and travelled to Spain and Corfu.

At the end of December 1893 Elisabeth visited Madeira again on her way from Algeria. She again spent Christmas there and remained until early February 1894, although she had originally planned to stay only ten days. Constantin Christomanos, one of Elisabeth's Greek tutors, accompanied her during this stay. The Empress lodged at the newly-built Reid Hotel in Funchal, which she found greatly to her liking.

Austria's last emperor, Karl I, arrived at Madeira on November 19th 1921 to begin his exile. He lived at the Quinta do Monte, on the road from Funchal to Monte, and not at the Quinta Vigia, as is sometimes erroneously supposed. Karl died in his place of exile on April 1st 1922.

Reichenau on the Rax
– the Rudolf Villa

Elisaberh Hassmann

The south façade of the Rudolf Villa seen from the garden; recent photograph. Apart from the enclosing of the open gallery around the inner courtyard, few alterations have been made to the villa since it was built.

The Rudolf Villa in Reichenau, taken on August 21st 1861, on the Crown Prince's third birthday. On the balcony are Gisela and Rudolf with their nurse; photograph by Ludwig Angerer, from one of the empress's albums.

The forests in the Semmering area around Reichenau on the Rax had been reserved as an imperial hunting ground since 1853. In order to provide the aristocratic participants at the hunts with accommodation of a suitably high standard, the Waissnix brothers had a one-storeyed villa with an open-galleried courtyard built on the site of an old farmhouse known as »Auf der Waag«. Completed in 1857, the villa was designed by the Viennese architect Anton Hefft in the early Viennese Historicist style, as plans found recently by Robert Pap document.

Franz Joseph, who knew the area around Reichenau from his shooting expeditions, gave orders for the newly-completed villa to be rented for the summer for his two children, Gisela and Rudolf. At the end of July 1859 the children, accompanied by their governess Baroness Charlotte von Welden and a personal retinue, made their first visit to Reichenau to stay at the emperor's villa, which local people from then on referred to as the »Rudolf Villa«. In 1862 Elisabeth spent several

The little huntsman's house given to Crown Prince Rudolf on his third birthday. Gisela stands in the entrance to the hut while Rudolf looks out of the window; photograph by Ludwig Angerer, from one of the empress's albums.

Ground plan of the Rudolf Villa (printed in 1865); it matches the poorly-preserved original designs of 1856 discovered by

Robert Pap that also bear the name of the architect, the Viennese Anton Hefft, which was previously unknown.

The Villa Warrens in Payerbach where Elisabeth stayed in 1873. The villa was demolished for no apparent reason in 1945; wood engraving after a drawing by Jul. Siemering, 1873.

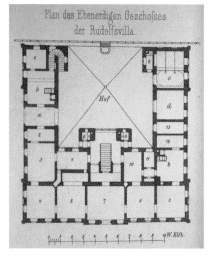

brief visits at Reichenau. On May 15th of that year, as she began her rest cure, she was so weak that she had to be carried into the Rudolf Villa on a litter. The crown prince's third birthday was also celebrated in Reichenau in 1862. When Rudolf turned six, the visits to Reichenau ceased. The villa became an annexe of the newly-built spa known as the Rudolfsbad. Today it is in private hands.

In 1873, the year of the World Exhibition in Vienna, Elisabeth recovered from her official duties relating to the exhibition (in whose performance, however, she had not been exactly zealous) at the Villa Warrens in Payerbach in the Reichenau valley. A newspaper article reported on her daily routine there: a morning constitutional in the park of the villa, clothed in a white morning gown and accompanied by her dog; occasionally an excursion on foot to Schwarza to fish. After luncheon she rested or worked at her desk. After dinner she rode or went for a walk. In the late evening she took a turn around the park again.

Bad Kissingen
– the spa resort of princes and the international beau monde
Elisabeth Hassmann

The »Arcade and Conversation« building in Kissingen was built in 1834–1838 under King Ludwig I after designs by Friedrich von Gärtner; historical photograph.

Elisabeth and her brother Carl Theodor at Kissingen in 1862; in the background is the hydro; heliotype.

Empress Elisabeth took the waters at Kissingen (known as Bad Kissingen from 1883) six times in all: in 1862, 1863, 1864, 1865, 1897 and 1898. As Elisabeth was still in poor health in the middle of 1862, despite having tried health cures at various spas and resorts, beginning with Madeira in 1860, Dr Fischer, her personal physician from Munich, decided that a health cure at Kissingen was the only remedy that would aid her recovery. The cure was so effective that Dr Fischer recommended the empress to make regular visits to Kissingen, advice which she duly followed. During her visit in 1863 she made friends with the blind Duke of Mecklenburg and the paralysed Englishman John Colett. On July 14th and 15th King Max II of Bavaria paid her a visit. In 1864 Elisabeth appeared at Kissingen accompanied by her husband. On June 19th 1864 they met the Russian emperor and his consort at the mineral springs promenade. King Ludwig II of Bavaria also visited Kissingen in 1864. During her visit in 1865 the empress was so bored that she

View of the Royal Hydro. Elisabeth stayed here in 1863, 1865 and 1897; copper engraving.

View of the villa Mon Bijou where Elisabeth stayed in 1898. It was demolished in 1970; historical photograph.

sent for her dog, Horseguard, to join her there.

The Prusso-Austrian war of 1866 interrupted her visits to Kissingen, and she was not to return there again until 1897. However, as on her previous visits, the waters did her good, and she repeated her visit the following year. The empress wrote to her daughter Valerie: »It is not greatly beautiful, but so charming, so good and so peaceful.« (quoted from Corti).

Elisabeth resided at three different places during her stays at Kissingen, none of which are still standing today. Initially, in 1862 and 1864, she stayed at the Carl von Hess Hotel in the Kurhausstrasse, which was demolished when the Victoria Hotel was built. The empress stayed several times at the Royal Hydro, in 1863, 1865 and 1867.

This building was originally designed by Balthasar Neumann in 1738, but had been extended and partially rebuilt in subsequent years. Today the Steigenberg hydro stands on the same site. On her last visit in 1898, Elisabeth took a whole floor in the Villa Mon Bijou, which stood at the foot of the Altenberg mountain. The villa was used as an annexe by the Diana Hotel but was demolished in 1970. The site is today used as a lawn for sunbathing.

In memory of the empress a monument was erected on the Altenberg mountain, where Elisabeth was fond of walking.

Trauttmansdorff Castle near Merano
Elisabeth Hassmann

Ansicht von Meran.

Elisabeth first visited Merano in October 1870, on the recommendation of Dr Widerhofer. Her daughter, Marie Valerie, had a weak constitution and he felt that a stay here would be advantageous. The empress remained at Merano until the beginning of June 1871 and resided at Trauttmansdorff Castle near Obermais. Her sisters Marie and Helene were also staying in Merano at the time. Elisabeth's second visit lasted from October 1871 to May 1872, with interruptions. This time she stayed at Rottenstein Castle. Seventeen years later, in the autumn of 1889, Elisabeth again resided at Trauttmansdorff Castle. On her fourth and last visit to Merano in September 1897, the empress went on a grape diet and stayed at the Kaiserhof Hotel (today a hotel management and catering college). As in the case of Cap Martin, Elisabeth's visits here made Merano famous throughout Europe.

Trauttmansdorff Castle is built around the remains of a 14th-century fortress known by the name of Neuberg. When Count Josef Trauttmansdorff acquired the ruined fortress in 1847, he rebuilt large parts of it: the walls of the medieval Great Hall were encased, the east wings extended and raised by a storey, a neo-Gothic chapel was built in 1853, and a courtyard laid out. The four-storeyed south wing terminates in battlements while the south-east wing, which is lower, has bow windows. The outward appearance of the castle today has hardly changed, whereas of the interior furnishings and decorations dating from that time only items such as tiled stoves, panelling and a few frescoes still remain.

At the time when Elisabeth was staying at Trauttmansdorff Castle it was owned by Moritz Ritter von Leon, who had acquired it in 1867. Extensive

Far left: tableau with views of the places stayed at by the empress and her retinue in 1870/71: Trauttmansdorff Castle, Rubein Castle, Villa Stadlerhof and Ramnetz Castle. The small roundel at the top shows Elisabeth with a small dog, perhaps the one she bought spontaneously from a passer-by on her arrival; wood engraving after a drawing by Franz Kollarz.

Trauttmansdorff Castle from the south; watercolour formerly owned by the empress, signed and dated Harveng, 1870 (Historical Museum of the City of Vienna).

This bathroom is the only room to have been preserved with its interior fittings as they were when Elisabeth stayed at the castle; photograph.

preparations were made for Elisabeth's first visit. The empress and Valerie occupied the south wing of the castle, while her elder daughter Gisela stayed at the nearby Stadlerhof. Several estates near the castle were rented for the empress's 106-strong retinue. These were linked to each other by telegraph, with a special telegraph office being set up at Trauttmansdorff Castle, which was connected to the palace in Vienna. The empress took such a liking to Trauttmansdorff that Franz Joseph, who visited her there several times, even considered buying it.

Gisela wrote to her brother Rudolf on October 17th 1870 that Trauttmansdorff Castle was a good place to play at being ghosts. Elisabeth once even had a giantess weighing 200 kilos brought to the castle from a showbooth in Merano in order to entertain her children and staff.

The castle has been in the possession of the Italian province of Alto Adige–Trentino since 1975. Following years of deliberation while the castle stood empty, it was recently decided to set up a museum of tourism there and lay out botanical gardens around it. According to research by Renate Abram (Merano) the only room that has been preserved as it was at the time of Elisabeth's visits is a bathroom. The memorial monument erected in honour of the empress in the garden no longer exists.

Bad Gastein
– the Empress's visits to the spa resort
Laurenz Krisch

Archduke Johann's villa in Bad Gastein (1851), later known as the Meranhaus, where Elisabeth stayed when she took the waters in 1886; pencil drawing by Anton Stern, a pupil of Georg Petzolt (Museum Carolino Augusteum, Salzburg).

Empress Elisabeth's visits to Gastein took place at a time when there was no railway connection with the spa resort, which then numbered only 1,400 inhabitants, a quarter of today's population. Although only about 7,000 visitors came to Gastein between 1885 and 1893, they included many of the crowned heads of Europe such as the German emperor Wilhelm I and the Austrian emperor Franz Joseph I, whose frequent encounters there contributed considerably to Gastein's rise to fame as a fashionable spa resort.

Elisabeth's first visit to Gastein was made in the company of her husband in 1885, when the couple stayed at the Straubinger Hotel, right beside the famous waterfalls.

The following year she took a cure at the Meranhaus hydro, which Archduke Johann had built for himself and his wife between 1828 and 1830. In 1926/27 it was extensively altered and converted into a hotel with 32 rooms and 45 beds. Its outward apperance has remained unchanged since this time. The present owner is Dr. Johannes Meran, the great-grandson of Archduke Johann.

In the years 1888, 1889, 1890, 1891 and 1893 Empress Elisabeth stayed at the Villa Helenenburg, where she particularly appreciated the peacefulness and seclusion. She also had the curative thermal spring water brought to the villa in wooden tubs on horse-drawn carts. Since she disliked having strangers around her and preferred to be unobserved, she rented the whole villa, which was more secluded than the hotels in the centre of the town. Her need for quiet went so far that from 1891 she even had one of the rooms at the villa converted into a chapel and summoned the local priest to celebrate mass there.

Apart from taking daily thermal baths, Elisabeth went on long hikes in the surrounding area, often in the company of her husband and her daughter, Marie Valerie. The empress always went on the more ambitious mountain hikes, such as on the Radhausberg (2,613 metres) or the Gamskarkogel (2,467 metres) with the local mountain guide Rupert Hacksteiner, as can be seen from entries in his mountain guide register. Emperor Franz Joseph (who stayed at the Meranhaus) mentions these hikes in a letter

Elisabeth stayed at the Villa Helenenburg in 1888, 1889, 1890, 1891 and 1893. She greatly appreciated the peaceful, secluded position of the villa, so much so that the emperor even considered purchasing it; postcard, c. 1920/25.

Empress Elisabeth's signature in the register belonging to the mountain guide Rupert Hacksteiner, who accompanied the empress on all her longer mountain hikes in the area surrounding Gastein.

to Katharina Schratt dated July 4th 1891: »I was not permitted to enter the Helenenburg before 9 am, since the empress had only come back from the Gamskaarkogel, a very high mountain with a celebrated view, shortly before my arrival, and was busy having a bath. She had started out at 11 o'clock in the morning the day before yesterday in this terrible heat with Countess Mikes and that Greek, accompanied only by a guide [Rupert Hacksteiner], and was intending to return by the evening. On the summit she was surprised by a thunderstorm and had to spend the night on hay in an alpine hut. For food she had only milk the whole day.«

In her remaining free time Elisabeth composed poetry such as the long poems *Gastuna* and *Windischgrätzhöhe*, which have been preserved in the Swiss Federal Archives in Berne since 1951.

The Villa Helenenburg, which was named after its former owner, Princess Helene Czetwertinsky, was built in 1867. When it was put up for sale in 1891, Franz Joseph considered buying it, »for a house in such a good situation and answering to all requirements is not to be had in Gastein any more«, opined the emperor. Since 1907 the villa has been owned by the motherhouse of the Protestant deaconesses in Gallneukirchen, near Linz. Turned into a field-hospital for the German Luftwaffe in 1944, the villa burnt almost to the ground the following year as a result of carelessness on the part of the soldiers quartered there. After various alterations, today the Helenenburg Kurhotel with its 52 rooms and 77 beds has regained all its old splendour.

Im memory of the empress's frequent sojourns at Bad Gastein a monument was erected in 1902 at the start of the promenade bearing her name which leads from Bad Gastein to Böckstein along the banks of the River Ache.

Cap Martin
– winters on the Côte d'Azur

Elisabeth Hassmann

Whenever the emperor wished to spend time with his consort, he often had no alternative but to follow her to wherever she was currently staying. One of the places where they met up was Cap Martin, which lies on the Mediterranean coast of France between Monaco and Menton. The place had been put on the map when Empress Eugénie of France had the Villa Cyrnos built there. When Empress Elisabeth began to spend the winter months at Cap Martin from 1894 to 1897, it became world-famous.

In 1888 the thickly-wooded headland was opened up by two roads and the Hôtel du Cap Martin built, where the empress was later to reside. Elisabeth and her retinue occupied the *piano nobile* on the mezzanine floor of the west wing, which had a total of 23 rooms. The empress had three rooms, one of which had a veranda that could be closed off with curtains. The adjoining three rooms were reserved for Franz Joseph. The reception room of the empress, like everything else in the Cap Martin Hotel, was elegantly distinguished and contained a brown satin damask divan and easy-chairs. In her bedroom were a writing-desk, a wardrobe with mirrors and a brass bed.

However, Elisabeth spent hardly any time at the hotel. She could leave the hotel grounds via a concealed entrance and thus avoid the numerous curious onlookers bent on catching sight of the empress. Security agents disguised as stone-breakers, postmen and so on kept the empress within sight at all times, however. Accompanied by her lady-in-waiting or her Greek tutor, Elisabeth undertook excursions in the immediate or further environs of the hotel. Prior to and after each long hike, the empress had herself weighed, despite the fact that she only consumed milk and eggs when out walking. These hikes were apparently so strenuous that Elisabeth sometimes had nosebleeds as a result (letter from Franz Joseph to Elisabeth dated March 24th 1894). In addition she visited the towns of Menton, Monte Carlo, Nice and Cannes.

The emperor visited his wife during each of her stays at Cap Martin. His visit in mid-February 1895 seems not to have been very pleasant. Franz Joseph remarked: »Our brief time together was truly sad in comparison to

Far left: Elisabeth (l.) and Empress Eugénie walking in Menton; photograph, 1895.

Exterior of the hotel on Cap Martin showing the west wing that was reserved for Empress Elisabeth; photograph, before/c. 1902.

The empress's reception room at the hotel; photograph, before/c. 1902.

The empress's bedroom at the Cap Martin Hotel; photograph, before/c. 1902.

what we had expected and hoped for« (letter of March 1st 1895). Elisabeth's longest stay on Cap Martin lasted from November 25th 1895 to March 15th 1896, during which she took a »Carlsbad Cure« (letters of December 6th 1895 and January 16th 1896), since she thought that at 50 kilos she was overweight. The emperor's third visit occurred in late February and March 1896, the fourth in March 1897. About the latter visit he remarked: »My stay at Cap Martin was completely spoiled for me by worry over the empress's health. My wife was so irritable that our time together was seriously disturbed« (quoted from Corti).

In February 1895 Queen Victoria came to Cap Martin. Meetings with Empress Eugénie were also unavoidable. Thus Elisabeth was not always able to withdraw completely from society when she stayed on the Riviera. After the empress's death a monument in the form of an obelisk was erected to her with an inscription making reference to her visits to Cap Martin.

Sassetôt
– a summer in Normandy
Elisabeth Hassmann

The empress's decision to spend the summer of 1875 in Normandy was the result of a recommendation by Elisabeth's personal physician, Dr Widerhofer, that her younger daughter, Marie Valerie, should bathe regularly in the sea to strengthen her weak constitution. Sassetôt-le-Mauconduit was chosen as their place of residence. This secluded 18th-century château lies approximately 12 kilometres from the railway station at Fécamp. Its owner at that time was one Albert Perquer, who wrote an account of the empress's stay there, giving a Marquis de Martainville as the owner, however.

Elisabeth arrived at Sassetôt on July 31st. The alterations to the apartments where the empress was to reside had begun only two days previously. She was given the ground floor rooms in the south wing, the salon also serving as her dining-room as well as a dressing-room. The iron bed she invariably used was transported in a black case. The room above her bedroom had to remain unoccupied so that nothing would disturb the empress's sleep. Elisabeth's *Obersthofmeister*, Baron Nopcsa, had rooms in the west wing. His apartments were directly accessible from the park, so that the empress would not be disturbed. Marie Valerie was put in rooms on the upper floor and had her own study where she took her lessons with her tutor, the prelate Hyacinth Rónay.

In order to provide for the empress's 70-strong retinue, a large herd of cattle had to be purchased. To the great joy of the local population, whose incomes were very low, immense quantities of food were bought for the imperial company's meals, which always consisted of six courses. The empress desired freshly-baked rolls to be served three times a day.

Rustimo, the little black boy whom Elisabeth had taken into her retinue to the horror of the court, had been taken along as company for little Marie Valerie, as had Elisabeth's huge grey mastiff, Shadow. The dog accompanied the empress everywhere during the day and at night it slept outside her bedroom door. A tall Nubian dressed in red had the exclusive task of caring for the dog.

Sea bathing and riding were Elisabeth's main occupations at Sassetôt. She had engaged a Swede as a swimming instructor and an Englishman named Allen as riding instructor. The bathing took place at Petites-Dalles,

Far left: View of Sassetôt by Anton Romako, who was a passionate admirer of the empress; watercolour formerly owned by the empress (Historical Museum of the City of Vienna).

Karl Reichert: portrait of the mastiff, Shadow, c. 1873. Greatly loved by Elisabeth, the dog was buried at Gödöllő; its gravestone still exists.

Sassetôt; recent photograph.

where a special wooden pavilion had been built as a bathing hut, from which a passage hung with draped cloth led to the sea, so that the empress could swim in privacy.

Her long rides across country led to disputes with the local population, since she often caused damage to fields and crops. The *maires* of the villages around Sassetôt were informed by Baron Nopcsa that any damage would be paid for. Perquer relates that Elisabeth also caused a sensation by allegedly riding out in the evening dressed in men's clothes instead of her usual tight-fitting riding-habit. It is said that she wore baggy breeches with grey suede gaiters. Occasionally she rode without a saddle, stretched out along the back of the horse.

On September 11th the empress suffered concussion after falling from her horse while jumping. She recovered, however, and did not have to have her famous knee-length hair cut off, as Dr Widerhofer had warned might be necessary. In 1914 Countess Caroline Zanardi Landi, who lived in America, claimed that this riding accident had only been a subterfuge:

Elisabeth had in fact given birth to a child and that child was herself, the so-called Child of Sassetôt. However, the countess gave her date of birth as 1882, which conflicts with the date of Elisabeth's stay at Sassetôt.

During her time at Sassetôt, Elisabeth commissioned a statue of her daughter Valerie from the sculptor Friedrich Salomon, then living in Paris, on the recommendation of the *Obersthofmeister*, Prince Hohenlohe. She was so pleased with the finished statue that she ordered another of herself. However, although several sittings took place, it was never completed due to Elisabeth's riding accident. According to Nolston the unfinished work remained at Sassetôt.

Elisabeth left Sassetôt on September 27th 1875 and travelled to Paris, where she resided at the Bristol Hotel. She never returned to Sassetôt. Today the château has been converted into a luxury hotel, but its outward appearance has not changed.

England and Ireland
– the empress rides to hounds
Elisabeth Hassmann

There is no doubt that it was Elisabeth's passion for riding that led her to make repeated journeys to England and Ireland. The fox and stag hunts there were the perfect setting for her to display her consummate skill and prove herself one of the best, if not the best horsewoman of her time. These hunting forays were undertaken between 1874 and 1882. After this period the empress, who suffered from increasingly severe rheumatism, visited England only for sea bathing.

Her first journey to England was to the Isle of Wight, where she arrived on August 2nd 1874 and took rooms at Ventnor. Elisabeth was accompanied by her little daughter Marie Valerie, as sea bathing was supposed to strengthen the child's constitution. When she visited London, Elisabeth caused quite a stir by riding out in Hyde Park. She also participated in cub-hunts, which take place before the regular hunting season begins. At the end of September she left the Isle of Wight.

The following year (1876) Elisabeth spent the summer riding at Sassetôt in Normandy.

In 1876 she travelled to England for the second time. The empress arrived at the beginning of March and rented Easton Neston, near Towcester in Northamptonshire, an estate that had formerly belonged to the Earl of Pomfret and was then owned by Lord John Spencer. Lord Spencer was Lord Lieutenant of Ireland at that time and was involved in the organisation of Elisabeth's journeys in England and Ireland. He resided nearby at Althorp Park, near Brington. A friend of his, Captain William George »Bay« Middleton, was engaged to accompany Elisabeth while out hunting. A friendship that was to last for many years developed between the empress and the officer, who was ten years her junior. The empress remained until the beginning of April. During her short stay she recovered her old spirits.

Her third stay in England started at the beginning of 1878. Elisabeth again resided near Lord Spencer's estate, this time taking a hunting lodge at Cottesbrooke. Her intrepidity while riding to hounds had increased to a point where she even found Middleton too cautious at times. Gossip about

Far left: the empress returning from a ride in Hyde Park. On her first trip to England Elisabeth did not take part in regular hunts; painting by Max Claude.

Above: Easton Neston, the Earl of Pomfret's estate near Towcester, where Elisabeth stayed in 1876; contemporary newspaper wood engraving.

Centre: Easton Neston, Northamptonshire, built in the early 1700s by Nicholas Hawksmoor, a pupil of Sir Christopher Wren, who had designed and begun building one of the side wings; photograph.

Below: »Bay« Middleton accompanied the empress hunting in 1876, 1878, 1879, 1880 and 1881; painting by Basil Nightingale (Borwick Collection).

the empress and Middleton proliferated and spoiled Elisabeth's stay, which she cut short in mid-February.

In the two subsequent years, probably at Lord Spencer's suggestion, Elisabeth hunted in Ireland, where in addition to fox hunts there were also stag hunts, a far more dangerous sport. Elisabeth took up residence in February 1879 at Summerhill Castle in County Meath, which belonged to Lord Langford. The reverence of the Irish for Elisabeth as a Catholic empress knew no bounds. Her elegant appearance was also much admired: she wore a close-fitting dark blue riding-habit with gold buttons and a tall hat. Elisabeth managed fences that brought even Middleton down. She was completely in her element, heedless of the serious affront that her visit to Ireland signified towards Queen Victoria and the enormous sums of money that her journeys entailed. Her stay in Ireland in 1879 cost over 150,000 gulden.

In February 1880 Elisabeth stayed at Summerhill again. She sent her husband detailed descriptions of the countless falls suffered by even the best riders. The emperor's concern for his wife was so great that he forbade her to make another hunting trip to Ireland, probably also for political reasons. Elisabeth was thus left no alternative but to travel to England again, although preparations for her stay at Kilkenny Castle had already been made.

On her third riding trip to England Elisabeth stayed at Cottesbrooke (Northampton-shire); photograph.

Elisabeth stayed at Summerhill, Co. Meath, in 1879 and 1880; photograph.

Combermere in Cheshire, built on the ruins of an abbey founded by Cistercian monks in 1130. Today only a few traces are left of the original buildings. Elisabeth stayed here in 1881 and 1882; coloured engraving, c. 1870.

Far right: Elisabeth and riders at a meet in front of Combermere Abbey. Elisabeth spent her last two hunting trips at Combermere; painting by an unknown artist.

Her fourth stay in England took place during February and March 1881. This time she rented Combermere in Cheshire, built on the ruins of a Cistercian abbey dating from 1130. The building that Elisabeth stayed in was known after its original owners as Cotton House. It was built in 1563 but had been extensively altered at the beginning of the 19th century in neo-Gothic style. Preparations made for Elisabeth's stay included the furnishing of a chapel and an exercise room, an obligatory feature of all the empress's residences. Electric bells to summon the servants were also installed. Her suite consisted of a drawing room with a bay window, a bedroom, dressing-room, bathroom and a waiting room for servants. A spiral staircase was built leading down to the kitchens so that Elisabeth could easily be served her frugal meals, which she preferred to take alone.

Elisabeth departed on her fifth and final visit to England at the beginning of February 1882. She again rented Combermere. Bay Middleton, who according to Marie Larisch, the empress's niece, had been constantly in Elisabeth's chambers on her earlier visits whenever they were not out hunt-

ing, was not part of the company this time. The empress obviously wished to avoid further gossip, especially as Middleton had announced his wedding for October. His successor as the empress's hunting companion, Major Rivers-Bulkeley, did not meet with Elisabeth's approval. For the first time she began to cancel rides and lost her pleasure in hunting. After a final meeting with Middleton the empress departed in great disappointment and ordered the horses in her English stable to be sold. With that, her »rushing about in England«, as her lady-in-waiting Marie Festetics put it, was over. Soon afterwards Elisabeth gave up fox-hunting and riding for good.

Miramar Castle near Trieste
– the residence of Archduke Maximilian, later Emperor of Mexico
Rossella Fabiani

Whenever Empress Elisabeth went on a sea voyage, she always began or ended the voyage at Miramar. On these occasions she was able to see various members of the imperial family who often stayed at Miramar, as is documented by the castle's visitors' book. Elisabeth's first visit to Miramar was made after her return from Madeira on May 18th 1861. She also stayed there with Franz Joseph in September 1882, on the occasion of the fifth centenary celebrations of the City of Trieste. The couple also spent Christmas 1889 at Miramar.

The castle is built of white Istrian limestone and consists of a ground floor, upper ground floor and mezzanine, together with a battlemented tower facing the sea. The ground plan of the castle is adapted to the natural form of the Punta di Grignano, the promontory on which it is situated, and consists of two main buildings connected to each other by a spacious stairway.

Built after a second set of designs by the Viennese engineer Carl Junker, the castle is a typical example of the style known as Romantic Historicism. Its models can be seen in the monumental buildings of the Vienna Arsenal by Theophil Hansen (built between 1849 and 1856) and the Arsenal in Trieste by Christian Hansen (completed in 1857), as well as the Villa Pereira in Greifenstein (Lower Austria) by Ludwig Förster and Theophil Hansen (1849).

The style of all these buildings derives from the school of Karl Friedrich Schinkel. His designs for Babelsberg Palace in Potsdam and Kurnik Palace in Poland founded the architectural style that inspired Carl Junker and Archduke Maximilian, who commissioned the castle at Miramar. Maximilian involved himself closely in the building of the castle and even drew up designs himself; however, these were for a considerably smaller, villa-type building.

Far left: Miramar Castle, built from 1856 by Carl Junker; recent photograph.

Junker's first set of designs were for a building with four storeys of which only three were eventually built (Archivio di Stato di Trieste, Fondo Miramare).

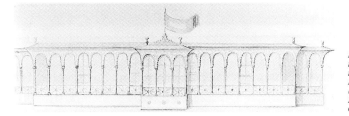

Design by Maximilian for Miramar, identified by Ferdinand Ander (Austrian National Library, the Maps Collection).

The gardens at Miramar, laid out by J. Laube and A. Jelinek, consisted of a formal, geometrically-arranged parterre and a more natural, romantic section. The zinc statues were a novelty; Maximilian wanted classical figures that would withstand the marine climate; photograph, before/c. 1872.

The furnishing and decoration of the castle, which was created by the Austrian interior decorators Franz and Julius Hofmann after Maximilian's instructions, corresponded to contemporary stylistic trends. The living and sleeping quarters of the archduke and his wife on the ground floor were done out in neo-Gothic and neo-medieval style between 1858 and 1860, while the state rooms on the upper ground floor completed in 1870 were decorated in neo-Renaissance and neo-Baroque and display all the typ-ical features of the second Austrian empire.

The private apartments of Maximilian and Charlotte on the ground floor are panelled in wood and have wall-hangings and curtains in azure blue embellished with a pineapple motif, symbolising wealth, together with a crown and anchor, the arms of a rear-admiral of the Austrian fleet. These interiors are imbued with the family atmosphere so typical of the Austrian Historicist style. From all the windows the archduke had a view of

Charlotte welcomes Elisabeth to Miramar on May 18th 1861 after the latter's return from Madeira. After Charlotte had left the palace for good on July 29th 1867, Elisabeth always occupied the apartments of her sister-in-law (whom she cordially disliked) on her visits to Miramar; painting by Cesare Dell'Acqua, 1864 (Miramar Castle).

Maximilian's study, known as the »Ship Room«; photograph by Stillfried, 1886. This room was designed as a replica of the officer's mess on the frigate »Novara« which Maximilian had captained on a voyage round the world in 1857-59.

Below: design for the archduchess's salon by Franz and Julius Hofmann. Maximilian gave instructions for his wife's rooms to be hung with blue silk.

the sea and could thus imagine that he was on board one of his ships.

After the tragic death of Maximilian on July 19th 1867 and the return of Charlotte to Belgium in a state of mental confusion from which she would never again emerge, the castle was used during the summer months by members of the Habsburg family. Following the outbreak of the First World War, all the furniture was transferred to Vienna, but was restored in its entirety in accordance with the terms of an agreement signed by Italy and Austria at the end of the war.

In 1929 the castle was opened to the public. Between 1930 and 1937 it was the permanent residence of Count Amadeo d'Aosta and his family, and during this period various changes were made to the interiors. During the Second World War Miramar was occupied first by the German army and then by Allied troops.

After the castle had been restored and refurnished with reference to contemporary paintings and photographs as well as sketches from Maximilian's album, it was reopened to the public as a museum on June 2nd 1955. Since this date, upwards of six million people have visited Miramar.

Garatshausen Castle on Lake Starnberg
– in the possession of Prince Thurn und Taxis
Gerhard Schober

Garatshausen today (photograph from 1992). The old castle is on the right, the new castle, now an old people's home, on the left.

The old castle of Garatshausen; watercolour dated 1854, formerly owned by the empress (Historical Museum of the City of Vienna).

Built by the Munich patrician Kaspar Weiler during the first half of the 16th century, Garatshausen Castle was purchased together with Possenhofen by Duke Max of Bavaria in 1834. However, it was then to remain uninhabited for 30 years. In 1867 Duke Max handed the castle over to his eldest son Ludwig, who sold it to his sister, Marie Sophie Amalie, the wife of King Francis II of the Two Sicilies, in 1871. In 1887 the castle then passed to the possession of her sister, Helene, who had married Prince Maximilian of Thurn und Taxis.

She had the castle renovated and the top floor converted into habitable space. Under Prince Albert further rooms were renovated and elegantly refurbished. At the same time, after the model of Possenhofen, a new wing known as the »New Castle« was built onto the west side. Today this is an old people's home run by the local authority. The castle itself, however, is still owned by the Thurn und Taxis family, who spend annual holidays here on the lake.

In 1868 and 1869 Empress Elisabeth spent her annual summer sojourns on Lake Starnberg at Garatshausen on the invitation of her brother Ludwig. In 1869 the visit lasted from July 4th to August 17th. Elisabeth and her daughter Marie Valerie lived in the castle, while their retinue and Duke Ludwig and his family moved into the adjoining wing. For their visitors' entertainment a wandering juggler and his dancing bear were engaged. Marie Louise, Duke Ludwig's daughter, was chosen as a playfellow for Archduchess Valerie.

The Strauch Hotel in Feldafing
– later known as the Empress Elisabeth Hotel – on Lake Starnberg
Gerhard Schober

The Strauch Hotel was built in 1856 by Joseph Anton Ritter von Maffei, the founder of one of Germany's oldest engine works. From its rooms and terrace the hotel commanded superb views of the lake and the alps beyond, as well as of the newly-opened Lenné Park.

In 1853 King Max II of Bavaria had commissioned the court director of gardens, Peter Joseph Lenné, to lay out an extensive park for a new palace on a tract of land bordering the lake. After the king's death in 1864, his successor, Ludwig II, ordered the semi-finished building to be demolished. The park, however, was completed after the original designs.

The Strauch Hotel became so popular during the next few years that an annexe had to be built in 1876.

It was during this period that Empress Elisabeth paid several visits to the hotel. The Strauch Hotel was not only furnished and equipped to the highest modern standards but also constituted an ideal starting point for her daily walks and rides. Every year since 1870 she had been in the habit of visiting her family at Possenhofen during the summer months. Court etiquette did not allow her to stay at the family home, and thus the Strauch Hotel was rented and closed to other guests.

The empress was mostly accompanied by her daughter Marie Valerie. They arrived on a special train together with a retinue of approximately 50 people (ladies-in-waiting and staff), who were accommodated in the annexe or in nearby private quarters, as well as several carriages and between 15 and 20 horses. For Elisabeth's personal use the neighbouring parsonage was also rented. A spiral staircase was installed in the hotel, allegedly because Elisabeth was afraid of fire. In 1882 a room was equipped for her with gymnastic apparatus and carpeted with mattresses. She took lessons in foil-fencing in the parsonage, or, if the weather was good, outside in the courtyard. She brought her own tableware with her, and of course her own kitchen staff. Elisabeth preferred simple meals; her favourite foods were milk warm from the cow and fresh eggs. Sometimes on one of her long hiking expeditions she would stop at a peasant's house for a meal. She rose very early and if the weather was good, she

Far left: the Strauch Hotel, enlarged by an annexe in 1876; photograph, 1885/90.

Above left: the hotel after further enlargement and its renaming as the Empress Elisabeth Hotel after her death; photograph, c. 1910/14.

Left: the Empress Elisabeth Hotel in 1988.

The statue of the empress executed by Karl Wilfert in 1905 which was removed from Franzensburg in 1918 and now stands in the gardens of the Empress Elisabeth Hotel.

would take a turn through the Lenné Park or walk over to Garatshausen. Frequently she would hike for hours, sometimes even as far as Andechs, several miles away over the mountains. When it was warm she enjoyed bathing in the lake; on these occasions the bathing establishment was closed especially for her. She frequently had herself rowed out onto the lake, often visiting the Roseninsel (Rose Island). After luncheon she would rest in a hammock in the parsonage garden.

Occasionally she was visited by her husband, Franz Joseph, or her son Rudolf, as well as her own relations, including Ludwig II, who always stayed at Berg Castle while Elisabeth was visiting. He would come on horseback, or sometimes cross the lake to the Roseninsel in his steamboat *Tristan.* If he happened to miss her there, letters would be left in a drawer of the writing-desk in the tower room of the villa on the island; these were the famous letters from the »Eagle« to the »Seagull«.

After the death of her son Rudolf, Elisabeth became increasingly unsociable and rarely went out. Her last visit to Feldafing was made in 1894.

In 1900, the hotel was permitted to change its name to the Empress Elisabeth in her memory, and in 1926 a white marble memorial to the empress was erected in the garden of the hotel. The monument had originally been created by the sculptor Karl Wilfert in 1905 for the spa resort of Franzensbad in western Bohemia. When the town decided to erase all references to the Habsburg dynasty in 1918, the monument was removed. Karl Wilfert, who had lived on Lake Starnberg since 1919, was instrumental in having the monument re-erected in Feldafing.

The Beau Rivage Hotel in Geneva
– Saturday, September 10th 1898
Elisabeth Hassmann

The coffin with Elisabeth's body leaving the Beau Rivage Hotel on September 14th 1898; photograph.

At the end of August 1898, Empress Elisabeth left Bad Nauheim, where she had been taking the waters, and travelled to Caux in Switzerland. From there she intended to pay several visits to various people, including Baroness Rothschild at Pregny on September 9th. After this visit, Elisabeth planned to spend the night in Geneva before travelling back to Caux. She therefore gave orders for rooms to be reserved under her usual incognito as the »Countess of Hohenembs« at the Beau Rivage Hotel, where she had stayed the previous year. She arrived with her lady-in-waiting in the early evening. They took a stroll together through the streets of the city and visited a confectioner's shop, eventually returning to the Beau Rivage towards ten o'clock. Elisabeth had taken suite No. 34–36 on the first floor, consisting of a large corner salon, a bedroom and another sitting room which had been hastily re-equipped as a bathroom for the »Countess of Hohenembs«. A bath tub and wash-stand had been set up and

the floor covered with oilcloth, which had been tacked to the floor. The room was decorated with armfuls of white asters. Countess Sztáray, Elisabeth's lady-in-waiting, was in the next room, and her other attendants on the floor above.

That night Elisabeth was unable to fall asleep until 2 am and slept badly for the rest of the night. However, the next morning she was in good spirits and left the hotel at 11 am together with her lady-in-waiting in order to make various purchases. She returned to the hotel soon afterwards as she was intending to catch the 1.40 pm lake steamer to Caux. The landing stage was close by the hotel and thus Elisabeth and Irma Sztáray did not leave the hotel until shortly before the ship was due to leave. They had walked about 200 metres when the Italian anarchist Luigi Lucheni ran into the empress, stabbing her with a file. Elisabeth was knocked to the ground by the impact, but had no suspicion of what had really happened to her. She was

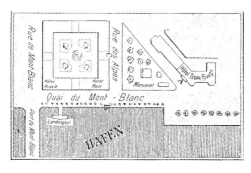

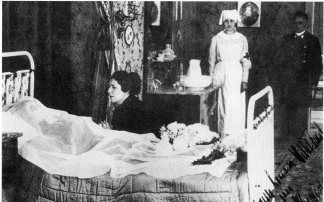

Diagram showing the scene of the crime:
A = the entrance of the Beau Rivage;
B = the place where the empress was fatally wounded, c. 200 m from A;
C = the place where Lucheni was seized; sketch after Heinrich Klingenberger, 1898.

Staged photograph: the empress on her deathbed, attended by Irma Sztáray. From the film »Elisabeth of Austria« (1920) by Rolf Raffé from a screenplay by Marie Louise Larisch-Wallersee, with Clara Nelson (empress) and Hedda Berger (Irma Sztáray). This picture is often erroneously taken to be an authentic photograph of the empress on her deathbed.

The empress's room at the Beau Rivage Hotel transformed into a chapel of rest; wood engraving after a photograph.

even able to board the ship but once there collapsed immediately.

Towards 2 o'clock the unconscious empress was carried back to her hotel suite on an improvised litter. The death certificate issued by the Geneva city authorities states: »Deceased at the Beau Rivage Hotel on September 10th at 2.10 pm in the afternoon.«

All the necessary steps were now taken in the room where the empress had died. First her body was dressed in a white shroud, then, on September 11th, a partial autopsy (of the thorax) was carried out and the corpse sub-

sequently embalmed. The body of the empress then was dressed in a black silk robe and her hair plaited into a crown. The physicians noted that the forehead and cheeks were yellowish in colour.

In the meantime arrangements had been made to turn the salon next door into a chapel of rest. The body of the empress was transferred there from the room where she had died and blessed by the Bishop of Freiburg, Mgr Deruaz. On September 14th the body was transferred to a coffin made by the imperial cabinet-makers which was then collected for the journey to Vienna. The carriage bearing the empress arrived the following evening. The hotel bed in which Elisabeth had died was also taken to Vienna but nothing is known of what subsequently happened to it. Today two portraits of the empress hang in the room where she died, commemorating her last visit there.

The yachts used by Empress Elisabeth – the *Fantasie, Miramar* and *Greif*

Wladimir Aichelburg

The »Fantasie«; historical photograph.

Depicting the empress on board a ship, this watercolour was executed by Leopoldine Ruckengaber after a photograph from 1897 on the express wish of Marie Valerie.

In contrast to Emperor Franz Joseph, who in general had a poor opinion of ships and sea voyages, Empress Elisabeth was bound by an almost fateful tie to travelling by ship and the sea. As a young bride she had arrived in Austria by boat and since that time hardly a year went by when she did not pace the deck of one ship or another. She fled by ship to Madeira during the first crisis in her marriage and it was on a boat that she was to die after having received the fatal blow from her assassin.

For Elisabeth ships were more than just a means of getting from one place to another; she adored being on boats of every kind and in every weather. She said to her Greek companion Constantin Christomanos in March 1882: »Life on board is more than mere travelling. It is an ameliorated, truer life. I try to enjoy it as fully and for as long as possible. [...] It is an ideal, chemically unadulterated, crystallized life, without desire or sense of time. The sensation of time is always painful, for it conveys to us the feeling of life.«

Apart from various smaller boats, it was in particular three yachts that were associated with the empress: the *Fantasie, Miramar* and *Greif.* All three were paddle steamers on which lengthy sea voyages could be made. At this time, fifty years after the invention of the marine screw propeller, paddle steamers were still preferred as passenger ships and yachts because they operated quietly. In the case of ships with screw propellers, the long propeller shaft caused constant vibration which was generally held to be unpleasant.

All three of these yachts were state ships, assigned to the Imperial-Royal Navy. Apart from the empress's voyages, they were used less for pleasure than for state purposes by high-ranking officials; on board these yachts state visits or inspections of the fleet were made and naval manoeuvres observed. In the event of war they could be used for reconnaissance, convoys, surveillance, troop transport or as accommodation for officers.

The oldest and smallest of the yachts used by Elisabeth was the *Fantasie.* Built between 1857 and 1858 by G. Rennie and Sons in London, it was commissioned by Archduke Ferdinand Max, later Emperor Maximilian of Mexico, who was at that time Commander-in-chief of the Austrian Navy. Fully equipped, the yacht had a displacement of 408 tonnes and was 55 metres long (59.50 metres in all) and 5.50 metres wide (10.40 metres across the paddleboxes); the steam engine had an indicated capacity of approximately 490 HP which gave the yacht a top speed of 13 to 14 knots. As was still usual at that time, two of the masts bore sail with a total surface area of 150 square metres. The crew consisted of two officers and 30 to 45 men according to requirements.

Delivery was taken of the yacht on May 7th 1858 and by July it had arrived in Venice where Archduke Ferdinand Max and his wife Charlotte joined the ship on its way to Dalmatia. During the following years the ship was stationed at Trieste. On May 18th 1861, Emperor Franz Joseph sailed to meet the empress who was returning from Madeira on board the British ship *Victoria and Albert.* They joined up off Pirano/Piran; Franz Joseph boarded the British ship and accompanied Elisabeth to Miramar, which at that time was still being built. Cesare Dell'Acqua later immortalised this episode in a painting which still hangs today at Miramar (ill. p. 140). After the turn of the century P. A. Sencig painted a copy of this picture for Archduke Franz Ferdinand of Austria-Este which is now at Artstetten Castle in Lower Austria.

The *Fantasie* was not only used for the private journeys made by the archdukes of Austria and the empress but also by the commander-in-chief for voyages along the Austrian coast. From 1887 it was also used as the flagship of the torpedo flotilla. In 1913 it was dropped from the fleet list and broken up for scrap.

The *Miramar* was designed by the imperial and royal naval architect Josef von Romako (brother of the painter Anton Romako, who made his reputation when the emperor bought his painting *Tegetthoff at the Battle of Lissa*). Fully equipped, it weighed 1,968 tonnes, was 82 metres long (92.70 metres in all), with a stern width of 10.40 metres, an indicated capacity of approximately 2,900 HP, a top speed of 15 knots and a total of 864.70 square metres of sail, with a crew of 144 men commanded by 14 officers. It was built by the Poplar company of Messrs. Samuda in 1871/72. The reason why an English shipbuilders' was again chosen was that the ship had been ordered specially for the emperor, and the naval high command did not want to risk any experiments with Austrian shipyards, which up to that date had little experience of yacht-building.

Because of its spacious interior, the *Miramar* was used frequently by the empress as well as Crown Prince Rudolf and later by Archduchess Marie Valerie for voyages in the Mediterranean. Between 1912 and 1915 it was in

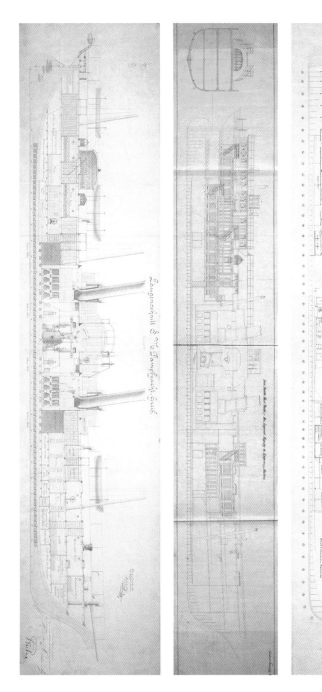

Longitudinal section
of the »Greif II«; plan
drawing (Kriegs-
archiv, Vienna).

Longitudinal section
of the »Miramar«;
plan drawing (Kriegs-
archiv, Vienna).

Longitudinal section
of the »Fantasie«;
plan drawing (Kriegs-
archiv, Vienna).

The yachts used by Empress Elisabeth

Photograph of Archduke Franz Salvator on the deck of the »Miramar« with Elisabeth under a parasol in the background; photograph, 1894.

The »Miramar« flying the imperial standard from the mainmast. When this drawing was made on April 20th 1875, Emperor Franz Joseph was on board, sailing from Trau (Trogir) to Spalato (Split); washed pencil and ink drawing (Historical Museum of the City of Vienna).

the senior reserve fleet, then it lay stripped at Pola and was finally assigned to Italy for scrap when the former imperial and royal fleet was divided up in 1920.

The *Greif* was built at Pola in 1882/83. It weighed 1,370 tonnes and was 73 metres long. It proved to be an extremely unserviceable vessel; after a mere thirteen years in service, the *Greif* was renamed the *Alpha* and converted into a hulk for the torpedo training school in 1896 before being eventually assigned to Italy to be broken up in 1920.

Originally the yachts were painted black on the stern, with a white superstructure and yellow smokestacks. It was not until 1885 that white became the usual colour for the whole ship. All three ships had two smokestacks each; the *Fantasie* had two masts, the *Miramar* and *Greif* three. The shape of the lateral paddleboxes was characteristic for all three of these yachts.

At 10.30 pm on April 2nd 1888, the *Greif* ran aground on the unlit island of Pago near Punta Koromacna as a result of a navigation error. Although the yacht ran onto a sharp reef at eight knots, the resulting leaks were insignificant and the incoming water managed by pumping. On board were the Crown Prince and his wife who had joined the ship shortly beforehand at Abbazia/Opatija.

An incident of this kind represented the worst nightmare of the naval officers responsible for the ship's safety. This time it had been an error in calculation which had led to the wrong course being set. However, it was mostly the empress herself in her passionate desire for freedom who often forced the officers into serious predicaments. She loved wild storms, when high waves came crashing down onto the ship's walls and flooded the decks. There are numerous accounts of the empress sailing through violent storms or wanting to sail in the smallest of boats.

The »Miramar«; historical photograph.

The saloon of the »Miramar«; historical photograph.

The empress's bedroom on the »Miramar«; historical photograph.

The yachts used by Empress Elisabeth

The »Greif«; historical photograph.

The goats were intended to provide milk for the empress to drink; historical photograph, c. 1890.

Ship's crew; historical photograph, c. 1890.

It was difficult to convince the empress of impending danger or the impossibility of her wishes; the emperor himself had expressly ordered that »absolutely no risks are to be taken in this respect, even if Her Majesty herself were thus inclined«. The officers did not want to appear indecisive or cowardly in front of the empress, but on the other hand they were fully aware of the added responsibility that rested on their shoulders when Elisabeth was on board.

The empress lived a modest and frugal life on board; she did not receive state visits or give official dinners. Nonetheless, her morning bath gave the captain headaches: so that the water would not slop out of the bath tub, the ship's course had to be changed or the engines stopped.

Then the goats that were supposed to provide milk for the empress, but dried up because of seasickness, had to be looked after. A Normandy cow that was also on board proved to have better sea legs. The quarterdeck where the empress spent her time outside was screened by sun canopies, and numerous pot plants had to be watered with fresh water every day.

Despite all this, Elisabeth was respected and worshipped by the crew; to have sailed with the empress was a great honour for any sailor.

The empress's royal saloon car and sleeping-car
Heinz Knauer

The history of the royal Austrian coaches and trains is bound up with the rise of the Austrian railways and goes back to the Biedermeier era.

On July 21st 1832, Emperor Franz II (I) and his wife travelled a short distance from the »mounting point« in Linz on the recently-completed horse-drawn railway between Linz and Budweis, the first railway to be built on the European mainland. This occasion was the first time a royal train had been used in Austria. However, except for the wheels, the »royal saloon car« had little in common with a railway carriage; it resembled rather an open car of the special mail coach.

The revolutionary innovation of the railway had started its triumphant progress in England and by 1830 was starting to spread to the continent. Financed with private capital, railway construction began early in Austria, and after the horse-drawn railway the first steam-driven train made its first journey on the first section of the Emperor Ferdinand Northern Railway in 1837. From 1841 the state also involved itself in railway construction. The various private railway companies subsequently surpassed one another in their efforts to provide the members of the imperial family and other important personages with comfortable saloon cars. The first proper royal saloon car, built on American models with four-wheel bogies by the Viennese firm of Heinersdorfer, was used on the state railway line between Olmütz and Prague; other companies soon followed suit. For journeys with a large retinue, several of these saloon cars from different railway lines were joined together. For shorter journeys two of these saloon cars sufficed, together with various accompanying coaches.

Far left: interior of Empress Elisabeth's royal saloon car. In the foreground is the dressing-room compartment, marked as »boudoir« in the plans. In the background is the sleeping compartment. The photograph shows the simple elegance of the interior colour scheme and the tasteful furnishings – an agreeable contrast to the overornate and ostentatious decoration of other coaches from the same period. The fittings were made by the Schönthaler Atelier, a studio for furniture and interior design in Vienna. The coach was originally lit by oil lamps, but was equipped with electric lighting in 1895, as can be seen from the switch beside the mirror and the two lamps with silk shades. The electricity was provided by a generator which was housed in a special lighting coach belonging to the royal train. In the centre of the doorway a candle-holder can be seen mounted on the far wall; this was for use in emergencies. The thermometer to the left of the mirror is decorated with a portrait medallion of the young Franz Joseph.

The royal saloon car, Hz 0011, of Empress Elisabeth, in the Museum of Technology, Vienna. The coach is painted a unobtrusive shade of green, which has darkened considerably due to weathering. During the 25 years it was in use, the coach was repeatedly adapted to new advances in technology and its tare weight increased from 13.5 t to 18 t. This increase resulted from the installation of a suction and vacuum brake, batteries for the electric lighting, which also served as buffers and were activated when the train was not in motion, as well as of steam heating. The suspended heaters for the original coal brick-hot air heating system can be seen between the first two wheels. To the right

underneath the first window is a small glass viewing panel for a thermometer, so that the train staff could check the interior temperature of the coach without disturbing the passengers and add fuel to the stoves if necessary.

The entrance vestibule contained the release mechanism for the emergency brake. This is equipped with the usual notice stipulating that it should only be used in emergencies, but without the otherwise usual warning of a fine in the case of improper use. No doubt it was felt that this was hardly appropriate for the saloon car of an empress.

Sleeping compartment of coach Hz 0011. The bed is on the left; on the desk to the right are writing utensils and a calendar. The windows could be blacked out completely and soundproofed by means of removable padded elements.

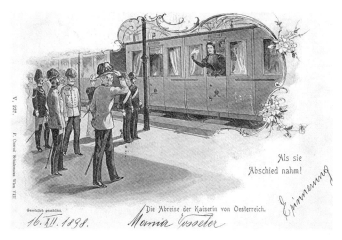

V. 287.

P. Conrad Schönborn Wien VIII

Gesetzlich geschützt.

16. XII. 1898.

Die Abreise der Kaiserin von Oesterreich.

Als sie Abschied nahm!

Erinnerung

Mama Vosseler

Elisabeth departing by train; commemorative postcard, 1898. The empress's preferred modes of transport were ship and train. She disliked travelling by coach, »for carriages make me nervous; one loses all one's identity thereby« (quoted in Nolston).

The imperial saloon cars from the early age of the railways were sumptuously decorated, with richly-gilded interiors, overladen ornamentation and garishly-coloured upholstery. The monarch's car was distinguished from the other coaches by imperial crowns mounted on the roof as well as splendid coats of arms and flamboyant decorations on the outer walls. After 1860 quieter colours were chosen and all grandiose ornamentation avoided, while great value was placed on the latest standards of technology.

The railway system expanded rapidly: the 130 kms of track for the horse-drawn railway (1832) had by 1870 become a network of 8,508 kms in the western half of the empire, with 5,375 kms in Hungary. At first the network concentrated on establishing north-south connections. Thus Duchess Elisabeth of Bavaria was not able to travel by rail to her wedding with Franz Joseph in 1854 since there was as yet no railway connection between Munich and Vienna. This was completed in 1860 and, in honour of the young empress and probably because of its connection with her beloved childhood home, it was named the Private Imperial-Royal Empress Elisabeth Railway.

In 1872, as a gesture of homage to their beloved empress, all the Austrian railway companies decided to join together to have a set of two saloon coaches built which would be presented to Elisabeth for her private use. The carriages were to be equipped to travel on all the tracks of neighbouring countries so that the empress could travel without delays. Thus the entrance steps, for example, could be folded up to fit the tighter Italian clearances. The fittings were to be in keeping with the empress's status, but kept plain, easy on the eye and without superfluous decoration, while at the same time being of the very highest quality. The set of coaches was built by the Ringhoffer company in the Smichov district of Prague and delivered in 1873.

In order to be able to to run on all routes, even those with small radius curves, the six-wheeled coaches had an outer wheelbase of just 4.43 m (later 6.45 m) and were only 9 m long (later 9.57 m). The coaches had a tare unloaded weight of 13.5 tonnes (later 18 tonnes). As the interior space was limited, the set consisted of a saloon and sleeper which were connected by a concertina gangway, still a very unusual feature at that time. The vehicles were maintained by the State Railway Company (despite its name a private company whose network was based at Vienna's Eastern Station) and were given the numbers 01 and 02.

After a royal train originally consisting of eight coaches had started operating in 1892, the empress's sleeping car (No. 02) was assigned to this train in 1895 and given the mark

Hz 0011 (Hz = Hofzug, i.e. court or royal train). At the same time maintenance was handed over to the imperial-royal Austrian State Railways (kkSTB), but like the whole imperial train, the coaches remained the property of the imperial court.

The reason why saloon car No. 01 was not assigned to the imperial train is not known; the coach has since disappeared without trace.

The operating log of imperial saloon car Hz 0011 contains the handwritten endorsement dated 1900: »Remains at the disposition of the *Obersthofmeisteramt* – not in service on grounds of piety«. Below this is an instruction from 1905 according to which the coach was donated to the Austrian Railway Museum, now part of the Museum of Technology in Vienna, where it is still to be found today. This preserved it from the fate of the rest of the imperial train, which had to be handed over to the victorious powers after 1918 and no longer exists.

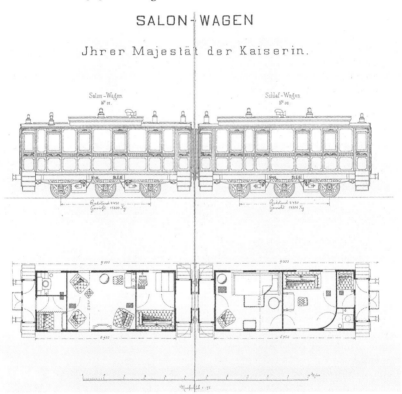

SALON-WAGEN

Jhrer Majestät der Kaiserin.

Salon-Wagen
Nº 01.

Schlaf-Wagen
Nº 02.

Registration document of the empress's two coaches from the period when they were maintained by the State Railway Company (StEG). On the left is the saloon car StEG No. 01, on the right the saloon car StEG No. 02, which was later to become the imperial saloon car Hz 0011. Today the interior of the coach largely corresponds to the plan, with the exception of the armchair in the servants' compartment which was replaced by a built-in cupboard for crockery. A remarkable feature is the flush toilet (marked as »Water Closet« in the plan), which was highly unusual at that time. Toilets in ordinary trains, if they existed at all, were located in the baggage compartment.

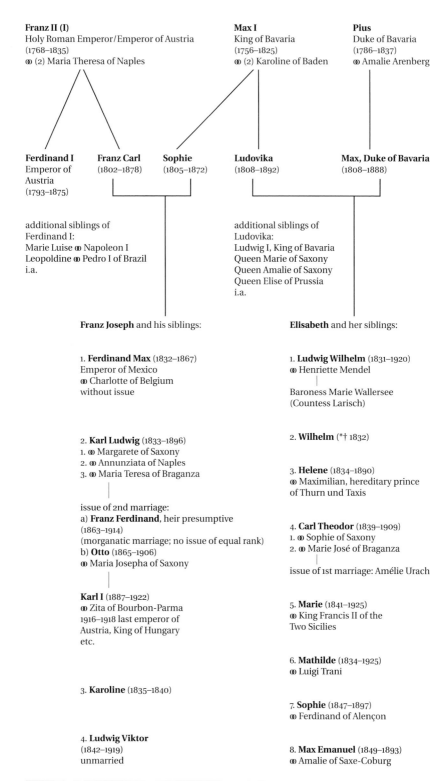

Franz II (I)
Holy Roman Emperor/Emperor of Austria
(1768–1835)
⚭ (2) Maria Theresa of Naples

Max I
King of Bavaria
(1756–1825)
⚭ (2) Karoline of Baden

Pius
Duke of Bavaria
(1786–1837)
⚭ Amalie Arenberg

Ferdinand I
Emperor of
Austria
(1793–1875)

Franz Carl
(1802–1878)

Sophie
(1805–1872)

Ludovika
(1808–1892)

Max, Duke of Bavaria
(1808–1888)

additional siblings of
Ferdinand I:
Marie Luise ⚭ Napoleon I
Leopoldine ⚭ Pedro I of Brazil
i.a.

additional siblings of
Ludovika:
Ludwig I, King of Bavaria
Queen Marie of Saxony
Queen Amalie of Saxony
Queen Elise of Prussia
i.a.

Franz Joseph and his siblings:

Elisabeth and her siblings:

1. **Ferdinand Max** (1832–1867)
Emperor of Mexico
⚭ Charlotte of Belgium
without issue

1. **Ludwig Wilhelm** (1831–1920)
⚭ Henriette Mendel

Baroness Marie Wallersee
(Countess Larisch)

2. **Karl Ludwig** (1833–1896)
1. ⚭ Margarete of Saxony
2. ⚭ Annunziata of Naples
3. ⚭ Maria Teresa of Braganza

issue of 2nd marriage:
a) **Franz Ferdinand**, heir presumptive
(1863–1914)
(morganatic marriage; no issue of equal rank)
b) **Otto** (1865–1906)
⚭ Maria Josepha of Saxony

Karl I (1887–1922)
⚭ Zita of Bourbon-Parma
1916–1918 last emperor of
Austria, King of Hungary
etc.

2. **Wilhelm** (*† 1832)

3. **Helene** (1834–1890)
⚭ Maximilian, hereditary prince
of Thurn und Taxis

4. **Carl Theodor** (1839–1909)
1. ⚭ Sophie of Saxony
2. ⚭ Marie José of Braganza

issue of 1st marriage: Amélie Urach

5. **Marie** (1841–1925)
⚭ King Francis II of the
Two Sicilies

6. **Mathilde** (1834–1925)
⚭ Luigi Trani

3. **Karoline** (1835–1840)

7. **Sophie** (1847–1897)
⚭ Ferdinand of Alençon

4. **Ludwig Viktor**
(1842–1919)
unmarried

8. **Max Emanuel** (1849–1893)
⚭ Amalie of Saxe-Coburg

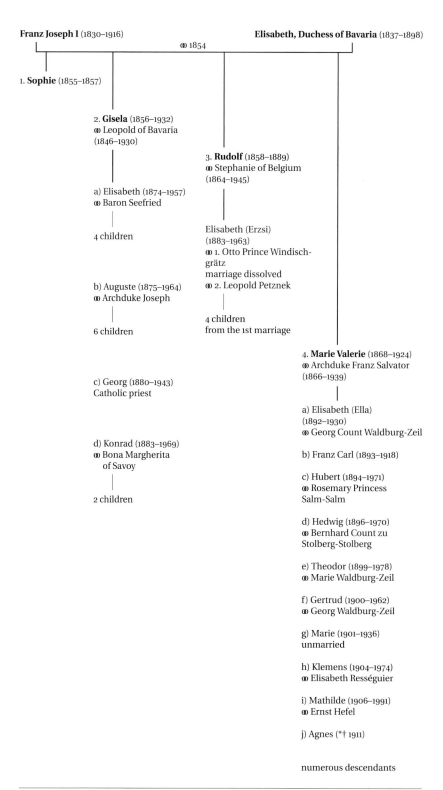

Franz Joseph I (1830–1916) ⚭ 1854 Elisabeth, Duchess of Bavaria (1837–1898)

1. **Sophie** (1855–1857)

2. **Gisela** (1856–1932)
⚭ Leopold of Bavaria
(1846–1930)

a) Elisabeth (1874–1957)
⚭ Baron Seefried

4 children

b) Auguste (1875–1964)
⚭ Archduke Joseph

6 children

c) Georg (1880–1943)
Catholic priest

d) Konrad (1883–1969)
⚭ Bona Margherita
of Savoy

2 children

3. **Rudolf** (1858–1889)
⚭ Stephanie of Belgium
(1864–1945)

Elisabeth (Erzsi)
(1883–1963)
⚭ 1. Otto Prince Windisch-
grätz
marriage dissolved
⚭ 2. Leopold Petznek

4 children
from the 1st marriage

4. **Marie Valerie** (1868–1924)
⚭ Archduke Franz Salvator
(1866–1939)

a) Elisabeth (Ella)
(1892–1930)
⚭ Georg Count Waldburg-Zeil

b) Franz Carl (1893–1918)

c) Hubert (1894–1971)
⚭ Rosemary Princess
Salm-Salm

d) Hedwig (1896–1970)
⚭ Bernhard Count zu
Stolberg-Stolberg

e) Theodor (1899–1978)
⚭ Marie Waldburg-Zeil

f) Gertrud (1900–1962)
⚭ Georg Waldburg-Zeil

g) Marie (1901–1936)
unmarried

h) Klemens (1904–1974)
⚭ Elisabeth Rességuier

i) Mathilde (1906–1991)
⚭ Ernst Hefel

j) Agnes (*† 1911)

numerous descendants

Bibliography and Sources

Sources used by more than one author

EXHIBITION CATALOGUE, *Elisabeth von Oesterreich. Einsamkeit, Macht, Freiheit*, 99. Exhibition at the Historical Museum of the City of Vienna 1986/87, Vienna 1986.

CHRISTOMANOS Constantin, *Tagebuchblätter*, 1st series, Vienna 1899.

CORTI Egon Caesar Conte, *Elisabeth.»Die seltsame Frau«*, 1st ed., Salzburg 1934 (numerous further editions some with different illustrations).

HAMANN Brigitte, *Elisabeth. Kaiserin wider Willen*, Vienna–Munich 1981 (revised ed. 1997).

HAMANN Brigitte, *Kaiserin Elisabeth. Das poetische Tagebuch* (Fontes rerum Austriacarum, 1. Abteilung Scriptores, 12. Band) Vienna 1995.

LEOPRECHTING Karl von, *Stammbuch von Possenhofen, der Insel Wörth und Garatshausen am Würmsee*, Munich 1854.

NOLSTON L. K. (pseudonym), real name KOHN Leopold (ed.): *Ein Andenken an Weiland Kaiserin und Königin Elisabeth*, Vienna 1899.

NOSTITZ-RIENECK Georg (ed.), *Briefe Kaiser Franz Josephs an Kaiserin Elisabeth*, 2 vols., Vienna–Munich 1966.

OTTILLINGER Eva B. – HANZL Lieselotte, *Kaiserliche Interieurs. Die Wohnkultur des Wiener Hofes im 19. Jahrhundert und die Wiener Kunstgewerbereform* (Museen des Mobiliendepots 3) Vienna–Cologne–Weimar 1997.

SCHOBER Gerhard, *Landkreis Starnberg* (Denkmäler in Bayern I.21) Munich–Zurich 1989.

ZIEGLER Peter, *Die ruhelose Kaiserin*, St. Michael 1981.

Imperial living, Eva. B. Ottillinger, p. 38–45

LOBKOWICZ Erwein, *Erinnerungen an die Monarchie*, Vienna–Munich 1989, 260f.

OTTILLINGER Eva B., Ein Stil für den Kaiser, in: *Kaisertum Österreich 1804–1848*, exhibition catalogue, Schallaburg 1996, 121–124.

VIRIBUS UNITIS, Das Buch vom Kaiser, ed. Max Herzig, Vienna–Leipzig–Budapest 1898, 4–11.

WITT-DÖRRING Christian, *Die abgelehnte Identität. Kaiser Franz Josefs private Wohnräume in Schloß Schönbrunn*, in: *Parnass* 1/1993, 92–96.

The Palace of Duke Max in Munich, B. Kuhn, p. 48–53

HEDERER Oswald, *Die Ludwigstraße in München*, Munich 1942.

HEDERER Oswald, *Leo Klenze. Persönlichkeit und Werk*, Munich 1964.

HEDERER Oswald, *Klassizismus*, Munich 1966.

KLENZE Leo von, *Sammlung architektonischer Entwürfe, für die Ausführung bestimmt oder wirklich ausgeführt*, I. Lieferung, Heft 1–4, Munich–Stuttgart–Tübingen 1830.

KUHN Barbara, *Vom Herzog-Max-Palais zur Landeszentralbank. Geschichte des Hauses Ludwigstraße 13*, published by the Landeszentralbank in Bayern, Munich 1990.

KUNSTBLATT, ed. Schorn, No. 48 (16th June 1828), No. 87 (29th October 1829), No. 97 (3rd December 1829), No. 82 (13th October 1835).

SCHAEFER Veronika, *Leo von Klenze. Möbel und Innenräume* (Miscellanea Bavariae Monacensia des Münchner Stadtarchivs 89) Munich 1980.

SCHWEIZER Korbinian, Vor hundert Jahren. Die Errichtung der Reichsbankhauptstelle in München – aus alten Akten, in: *Die Bundesbank*, No. 49 (March 1975) 6ff.

Possenhofen Castle/Lake Starnberg, G. Schober, p. 54–59

ECHTER Claus-Peter, *Beiträge zur Geschichte des Schlosses Possenhofen*, in: Oberbayerisches Archiv 105, Munich 1880.

SCHOBER Gerhard, *Bilder aus dem Fünf-Seen-Land*, Starnberg 1979.

SCHOBER Gerhard, *Prunkschiffe auf dem Starnberger See*, Munich 1982.

The Vienna Hofburg, Georg J. Kugler, p. 60–69

KUGLER Georg, *Franz Joseph und Elisabeth*, Florence–Graz 1994.

KUGLER Georg, *Wiener Hofburg. Die Kaiserappartements*, Vienna 1996.

SCHNÜRER Franz (ed.), *Briefe Kaiser Franz Josephs I. an seine Mutter 1838–1872*, Munich 1930.

The Blauer Hof at Laxenburg, E. Springer, p. 70–75

FOIST Johann – MARINOVIC Georg – SPRINGER Elisabeth, *Laxenburg. Chronik – Bilder – Dokumente. Ein Heimatbuch*, Mödling 1988.

HAUS-, HOF- UND STAATSARCHIV WIEN, Obersthofmeisteramt R. 43 for the relevant year; ceremonial protocol for the relevant year.

SPRINGER Elisabeth, Berthold der Landschreiber – Berthold der Schützenmeister. Der Laxenburger Kauf von 1306 und die frühen Habsburger in Österreich, in: *Jahrbuch für Landeskunde von Niederösterreich* (commemorative publication of the Verein für Landeskunde von Niederösterreich issued on the occasion of the Ostarrichi Millenium), Neue Folge 62 (1996) 293–318.

Schönbrunn Palace, Elfriede Iby, p. 76–85

HAJÓS Géza, *Schönbrunn* (Wiener Geschichtsbücher 18) Vienna–Hamburg 1976.

IBY Elfriede (ed.), *Schloß Schönbrunn: Zur frühen Baugeschichte* (Wissenschaftliche Reihe Schönbrunn 2) Vienna 1996.

RASCHAUER Oskar, Geschichte der Innenausstattung des Lustschlosses Schoenbrunn. Eine denkmalkundliche Darstellung mit besonderer Berücksichtigung der Mariatheresianischen Schönbrunn und mit Ergänzungen zur allgemeinen Baugeschichte des Schlosses, 2 vols., doctoral thesis, Vienna 1926.

SCHLOSS SCHÖNBRUNN KULTUR UND BETRIEBSGES. M. B. H. WIEN, Raschauer estate.

Imperial Dairy Farm/Schönbrunn, I. Haslinger, p. 86–87

BUNDESMOBILIENVERWALTUNG WIEN, Kammermeierei Inventar 1918.

HAUS-, HOF- UND STAATSARCHIV WIEN, Obersthofmeisteramt R. 134 und 75; Estate of Conte Corti K 13–16.

URBAN Leopold, Die Schönbrunner Kammermeierei in späten Jahren, in: *100 Jahre Gärtnerische Ausbildung in Wien. Gemeinsames Erbe*, Vienna 1995.

The Imperial Villa at Bad Ischl, M. Oberhammer, p. 88–91

EXHIBITION CATALOGUE, *Kaiser Franz Joseph I. und Bad Ischl*. Exhibition on the 150th anniversary of the birth of Emperor Franz Joseph I (1630–1980), organised by the Ischler Heimatverein.

OBERHAMMER Monika, Architektur des 19. Jahrhunderts in Ischl, in: *Oberösterreich. Kulturzeitschrift*, vol. 30, 3 (1980).

OBERHAMMER Monika, *Sommervillen im Salzkammergut*, Verlag Galerie Welz, Salzburg 1983.

The Hermes Villa at Lainz, Peter Haiko, p. 92–97

ALLGEMEINES VERWALTUNGSARCHIV WIEN, Stadterweiterungsfonds Fasc. 378, Varia.

HAUS-, HOF- UND STAATSARCHIV WIEN, Generaldirektion der Privat- und Familienfonde; Sekretariat Elisabeth, Index.

SCHNITZER Ignaz (ed.), *Franz Joseph I. und seine Zeit. Cultur-historischer Rückblick auf die Francisco-Josephinische Epoche*. Commemorative volume 1898, Vienna–Munich 1898, 99ff.

The Palace at Buda, Beatrix Basics, p. 98–103

EXHIBITION CATALOGUE, *Erzsébet a magyar királynéja – Elisabeth Königin von Ungarn*, Museum Österreichischer Kultur in Eisenstadt, Böhlau Verlag, Vienna–Cologne–Weimar 1991.

EXHIBITION CATALOGUE, A Városi Helytörténeti Gyüjtemény kiállítása Erzsébet királyne születésének 150. Évordulójára (Exhibition at Gödöllő marking the 150th centenary of Queen Elisabeth's birth) Gödöllő 1987.

FÖLDI-DÓZSA Katalin, Erzsébet királyné éreklyéinek története, in: *Erzsébet a magyarok királynéja (Elisabeth, Königin von Ungarn)*. Kiállítás a Magyar Nemzeti Múzeumban (exhibition at the National Museum of Hungary) Budapest 1992, 27–29.

GERŐ László, A budai vár helyreállítása, Budapest 1957.

HAUSZMANN Alajos, A magyar királyi vár, Budapest 1922.

MOJZER Miklós, Torony – kupola – kolonnád, Budapest 1971, 36, 46–47.

SZALAY Imre von, Az Erzsébet királyné emlékmúzeum Budapest, Budapest 1909.

ZAKARIAS Sándor, Budapest. Magyarország müvészeti emlékei, Budapest 1961, 41–44.

Gödöllő Palace, Ferenc Dávid, p. 104–109
DÁVID Ferenc, Königin Elisabeth und Gödöllő, in: Elisabeth Königin von Ungarn. Erzsébet a magyarok királlynéa, exhibition catalogue, Museum Österreichischer Kultur in Eisenstadt, Vienna–Cologne–Weimar 1991, 50–57.
HAUS-, HOF- UND STAATSARCHIV VIENNA, OMeA SR XII/2/155a.
RIPKA Ferencz, Gödöllő a király család otthona, Budapest 1896.

The Achilleion on Corfu, Ingrid Haslinger, p. 110–117
BUNDESMOBILIENVERWALTUNG VIENNA, Akten.
HAUS-, HOF- UND STAATSARCHIV VIENNA, Obersthofmeisteramt; Generaldirektion der privaten Familienfonde; Estate of Conte Corti; Politisches Archiv, Sekretariat der Kaiserin Elisabeth; Planmappe»Corfu Achilleion«; Journal Corfu.
HOLZSCHUH Robert (ed.): Die letzte Griechin. Die Reise der Kaiserin Elisabeth nach Korfu im Frühjahr 1892, erzählt nach den Tagebuchblättern von Constantin Christomanos, Eduard Krem-Bardischewski Verlag, Aschaffenburg 1996.
MAIER Michael, Achilleion (Große Baudenkmäler 179) Munich 1963.
WARSBERG Alexander von, Odysseeische Landschaften, Vienna 1878.
KAISER WILHELM II., Erinnerungen an Korfu, Berlin–Leipzig 1924.

Madeira, Elisabeth Hassmann, p. 120–121
FALKENAU Doris, Auf Sisis Spuren in Madeira,Vienna1996.
LIPPS Susanna, Madeira, Cologne 1992.

Reichenau on the Rax, Elisabeth Hassmann, p. 122–123
KOS Wolfgang (ed.), Die Eroberung der Landschaft. Semmering – Rax – Schneeberg. Katalog zur Niederösterreichischen Landesausstellung Schloß Gloggnitz 1992, Vienna 1992. esp. articles by Wolfgang Kos (S. 247) and Robert Pap (S. 477ff.).
PAP Robert, Wiedergefundenes Paradies. Sommerfrischen zwischen Reichenau und Wien, St. Pölten–Vienna 1996.
PAP Robert – PUSCH Eva, Reichenau an der Rax, St. Pölten 1988.
PUSCH Eva – SCHWARZ Mario, Architektur der Sommerfrische, St. Pölten–Vienna 1995.

Bad Kissingen, Elisabeth Hassmann, p. 124–125
HAHN Edi, Ein Führer durch die Kuranlagen, Bad Kissingen 1992.
SOTIER Alfred, Bad Kissingen, 2nd edition, Leipzig 1883.
STERZINGER Irmgard – STERZINGER Richard, Auf den Spuren von Kaiserin Elisabeth, Eigenverlag, Nürnberg 1996.

Trauttmansdorff Castle, E. Hassmann, p. 126–127
ELLMENREICH Albert: Meran als vornehmer Kurort, in: Bruno Pokorny, Meran, hundert Jahre Kurort 1836–1936, Innsbruck 1936, 40–51.
KINZ Thomas-Ernst, Sanatorium und Tagesklinik auf Schloß Trauttmansdorff/Meran, diploma thesis, University of Innsbruck 1990.
MAZEGGER B., Der Kurort Meran-Mais. Illustrierter Führer für Kurgäste, Verlag Woerl, 2nd ed., Leipzig 1899.
WEINGARTNER Josef – HÖRMANN-WEINGARTNER Magdalena, Die Burgen Tirols, 3rd edition, Munich 1981.

Bad Gastein, Laurenz Krisch, p. 128–129
BOURGOING Jean de, Briefe Kaiser Franz Josephs an Katharina Schratt, Vienna 1949.
KRISCH Laurenz: Die Kaiserin Elisabeth und ihr Bergführer Rupert Hacksteiner, in: Gästezeitung Gasteinertal, October/November 1995.
KRISCH Laurenz, Kaiserin Elisabeth und ihre Gastein-Gedichte, in: Gästezeitung Gasteinertal, July 1996.
LEBOUTON Ekkehart, Die Lutherischen in der Gastein, Vienna 1962.
ZIMBURG Heinrich, Die Geschichte Gasteins und des Gasteiner Tales, Vienna 1948.

Cap Martin, Elisabeth Hassmann, p. 130–131
CLAUD-SAAR Anna, Kaiserin Elisabeth auf Kap Martin, Zurich 1902.

Sassetôt, Elisabeth Hassmann, p. 132–133
DESCARS Jean, Sur les pas de Sissi, Paris 1989.
PERQUER Albert: Une Villégiature impériale en Pays de Caux, Paris 1897.

England and Ireland, Elisabeth Hassmann, p. 134–137
MEE Arthur, Northamptonshire, London 1945, 107ff.
SOKOP Brigitte: Jene Gräfin Larisch. Marie Louise Gräfin Larisch-Wallersee. Vertraute der Kaiserin – Verfemte nach Mayerling, 3rd rev. ed., Vienna–Cologne–Weimar 1992 (1. ed. 1985).
WEISSENSTEINER Friedrich: Lieber Rudolf. Briefe von Kaiser Franz Joseph und Elisabeth an ihren Sohn, Vienna 1991.
WELCOME John, Die Kaiserin hinter der Meute. Elisabeth von Österreich und Bay Middleton, Vienna–Berlin 1975.

Miramar Castle near Trieste, R. Fabiani, p. 138–140
FABIANI Rossella: Schloß Miramare. Das historische Museum, Trieste 1989.
HAUS-, HOF- UND STAATSARCHIV WIEN, Handwritten monograph on Miramar Castle, undated (c. 1872/73), Sign. OMeA SR XII/2/155.
RUARO LOSERI Laura (ed.), Maximilian von Triest nach Mexiko, exhibition catalogue, Trieste 1986.
RUARO LOSERI Laura (ed.), Massimiliano. Rilettura di un'Esistenza, Trieste 1987.
WELLER Franz: Die kaiserlichen Burgen und Schlösser in Bild und Wort, Vienna 1880.

The Strauch Hotel in Feldafing, G. Schober, p. 142–143
KISTLER Ferdinand, Heimatbuch für Feldafing, 1929 (typewritten ms., Feldafing 1990).

The Beau Rivage Hotel/Geneva, E. Hassmann, p. 144–145
BANKL Hans, Krankengeschichte und Obduktionsbefund der Kaiserin Elisabeth von Österreich (1837–1898), in: Mitteilungen des Pathologisch-anatomischen Bundesmuseums in Wien, 1 (1989) 15–30.
DORFMEISTER F. A., Kaiserin Elisabeth von Oesterreich. Eine Schilderung des Lebens, Wirkens und Sterbens unserer unvergesslichen Kaiserin, Vienna 1898.
KLINGENBERGER Heinrich, Kaiserin Elisabeth von Österreich, Vienna 1898.
MATRAY Maria – KRÜGER Answald, Der Tod der Kaiserin Elisabeth oder Die Tat des Anarchisten Lucheni, Munich–Vienna–Basel 1970.
N. N., Die Ermordung der Kaiserin Elisabeth von Oesterreich am 10. September 1898, Vienna 1898.
SZTÁRAY Irma, Aus den letzten Jahren der Kaiserin Elisabeth, Vienna 1909.

Yachts, Wladimir Aichelburg, p. 146–151
AICHELBURG Wladimir, K. u. k. Dampfschiffe, Kriegs-, Handels- und Passagierschiffe in alten Photographien, Verlag Orac, Vienna 1982 (new edition Österreichische Staatsdruckerei, Vienna 1996).
AICHELBURG Wladimir, K. u. k. Yachten und Yachtclubs Österreich-Ungarns in alten Photographien, Verlag Orac, Vienna 1986 (new edition Österreichische Staatsdruckerei, Vienna 1996).
MARINE GESTERN – HEUTE, No. 1 (1980) 24–25, No. 1 (1988) 24–17.
N. N., Festschrift on the occasion of the unveiling of the monument to Empress Elisabeth in Trieste, special supplement of the Triester Tagblatt, Trieste 1912, 16–18, 20–21.
YACHTREVUE, No. 4 (1980) 90–92, No. 6 (1980) 76–79, No. 7 (1980) 76–78, No. 2 (1981) 54–56.

Royal saloon car and sleeping-car, H. Knauer, p. 152–155
DOST P., Der rote Teppich, Stuttgart 1956.
RÖLL V., Hofzüge (Enzyklopädie des Eisenbahnwesens 6) Urban & Schwarzenberg, Berlin–Vienna 1914.
STRACH H., Wagenbau (Geschichte der Eisenbahnen der österreichisch-ungarischen Monarchie 2) Vienna–Teschen–Leipzig 1898.
TECHNISCHES MUSEUM VIENNA, Archiv Österreichisches Eisenbahnmuseum.

Illustration credits

The numerals refer to page numbers.
abbreviations used:
l: left, c: centre, a: above, r: right, b: below.

Photographers:
F.I.: Faludi Ildikó, Budapest
H.M.: Haller Marianne, Perchtoldsdorf near Vienna
O.U.: Otto Udo, Vienna
T.G.: Trumler Gerhard, Vienna
W.J.: Wagner Johannes, Vienna

Academy of Fine Arts, Vienna, Kupferstichkabinett:
111/a, 111/b (Peter Semrad, Vienna)

Anrather Oskar, Salzburg: 88/b

Archivio di Stato di Trieste, Fondo Miramare:
139/a (E. Halupca), 140/b (M. Ierman, Linea Museo)

Austrian National Library, Vienna, Bildarchiv- und
Portraitsammlung:
9/ar, 10/l, 11, 16, 18/l, 19/ar, 19/b, 21, 23, 25/b, 26/a,
26/b, 28/l, 28/r, 29/r, 32, 43/a, 43/c, 47/a, 56/b, 58/a,
62/a, 63/a, 63/c, 64/a, 64/c, 64/b, 66, 67, 69/b, 84, 88/a,
89, 91/a, 91/bl, 91/br, 95/a, 95/b, 96/alle, 99/a, 100/c,
100/bl, 106/a, 107/a, 107/b, 109/a, 109/b, 110/a, 113,
116/l, 116/r, 119/a, 119/cb, 120/b, 124/b, 125/b, 126,
130, 134, 136/b, 137, 140/c, 144, 145/c, 145/b, 153/b

Austrian National Library, Vienna, Kartensammlung:
139/c

Bayerisches Landesamt für Denkmalpflege, Munich:
51/a, 51/b

Bergbau- und Heimatmuseum, Reichenau:
123/bl (Rudolf Pap, Payerbach)

Biczó Tamás (Corvina Verlag, Budapest): 100/a

Bildarchiv Preussischer Kulturbesitz, Berlin: 46/cb

Bötsch Josef, Bad Kissingen: 125/a

Casa Editrice B & MM Fachin, Bruno Fachin, Trieste:
138 (M. Marin)

Federal Swiss Archives, Berne: 25/a

Gödöllő Királyi Kastélymúzeum:
104 (F.I.), 105/b, 106/b (F.I.), 108/al (F.I.), 108/ar (F.I.)

Graphische Sammlung Munich:
47/ca (Christine Pahnke, Munich)

Habsburg-Lothringen Michael, Persenbeug: 149/a

Halama Dieter, antiquarian bookshop, Vienna:
102/a, 102/c

Haslinger Ingrid, Deutsch-Wagram:
86 (Rudolf Meidl, Deutsch-Wagram), 110/b

Haus-, Hof- und Staatsarchiv, Vienna:
14/a, 62/b, 71/a, 87/a, 112/a, 112/b, 139/b (O.U.)

Heinemann Paul, antiquarian bookshop, Starnberg nr.
Munich: 46/a, 112/c, 118/ca, 121, 135/a

Historical Museum of the City of Vienna:
12/a (O.U.), 13, 15 (O.U.), 17, 18/r, 20 (O.U.), 27, 45/al,
46/c, 47/cb, 61/b, 72, 74/b, 78/b (Rudolf Stepanek,
Vienna), 92/a, 92/b, 94/a, 95/b, 105/a, 108/b (O.U.),
118/b (O.U.), 124/a, 127/a, 132, 133/a, 141/b (O.U.),
149/b

Holzschuh Robert, Aschaffenburg:
31/r, 47/c, 63/b, 118/a

Kabelka Viktor, Vienna: 30, 114, 115/a, 151/bl, 151/br

K. k. Schlösser Artstetten und Luberegg, Artstetten:
38 (Fritz Simak, Vienna)

Klosterneuburg Augustinerchorherrenstift:
inside front cover (Sign. J III 270 b), 70

Kriegsarchiv, Marinereferat, Vienna:
146/a, 148 (all), 150 (all), 151/a

Krisch Laurenz, Bad Gastein: 119/ca, 129/a, 129/b

Kunsthistorisches Museum, Vienna:
7/a, 7/c, 19/al, 79, 80/a

Landeszentralbank im Freistaat Bayern, Munich:
50/al, 50/ar, 52/a, 53

Münchner Stadtmuseum, Graphiksammlung:
9/al, 47/b, 49/a, 49/b, 52/b, 54, 55/b, 57

Museen des Mobiliendepots, Vienna:
31/l (H.M.), 39 (H.M.), 45/ar, 82/a, 87/b (H.M.)

Museo Storico del Castello di Miramare, Trieste:
140/a (G. Iosini)

Museum Carolino Augusteum, Salzburg: 128

Museum of Hungarian Architecture, Budapest:
106/c (F.I.)

Museum of Tourism Trauttmansdorff Castle, nr.
Merano: 127/b

National Museum of Hungary, Budapest:
7/b, 98, 99/c, 99/b, 100/br, 101

Neff Paul Verlag, Vienna–Berlin:
135/c, 135/b, 136/a, 136/c

Niederösterreichische Landesbibliothek St. Pölten,
Topographische Sammlung: 123/br

Palais Schwarzenberg, Vienna: 71/b

Pap Robert, Payerbach: 122/a

Perrin Verlag, Paris: 90/a, 90/b (all Jérôme da Cunha),
120/a, 133/b (Jérôme da Cunha)

Private collections: 48, 50/b, 52/c, 56/a, 68, 142,
143/al (Gerhard Schober, Ganting), 146/b (Sotheby's)

Rebasso, Vienna: 9/b (W.J.)

Sacher Hotel, Vienna: 6/a, 14/b (W.J.)

Schloss Laxenburg Betriebsges. m. b. H., Laxenburg:
74/a, 74/c, 75 (all Franz Karl Nebuda, Ebreichsdorf)

Schloss Schönbrunn Kultur- und Betriebsges. m. b. H.,
Vienna: frontispiece (W.J.), 10/r (W.J.), 12/b, 22/a, 22/b,
41 (T.G.), 43/b (H.M.), 45/c, 45/b, 46/ca, 46/b, 58/b,
60 (W.J.), 61/a, 69/a (H.M.), 73/a, 73/b, 76/a (T.G.),
76/b (W.J.), 77 (W.J.), 78/a (W.J), 78/c (W.J.), 80/b (T.G.),
81 (T.G.), 82/b (T.G.), 83, 85/l (W.J.), 85/r (W.J.), 102/b,
115/c, 115/b, 117/a, 117/b, 119/b, 131/a, 131/bl, 131/br,
145/a, 154

Schober Gerhard, Ganting:
55/a, 59/a, 59/b, 141/a, 143/ar, 143/b

Széchényi Library, Budapest: 29/l

Technisches Museum, Vienna: 152 (O.U.), 153/a, 155

Thurn und Taxis, Fürstliche Kunstsammlung, Regensburg: 6/b

Wallraf Richartz-Museum Cologne, Agfa Foto-
Historama: 122/b, 123/a

Wittelsbacher Ausgleichsfonds, Munich: 6/c, 118/cb

Zentralinstitut für Kunstgeschichte, Munich: 8